Your Pets, *and You*

🕷

THE AUTHORS

George Hendry (PhD, DSc) is a biochemist, an ecologist, a university reader and author of over 150 original research papers and books. He also wrote the bestselling book *Midges in Scotland* on another of Scotland's little charmers. The sight of his four-year-old daughter coming in from the garden with fourteen ticks spurred him to link up with...

Darrel Ho-Yen (BMSc (Hons), MB, ChB, FRCPath, FRCP, MD, DSc), Head of Microbiology, NHS Highland, Director of the Scottish Toxoplasma Reference Laboratory and honorary clinical senior lecturer at Aberdeen University. He is the author of over 100 original research papers and several books. The Department at Raigmore Hospital provides a specialist diagnostic service for Lyme disease in Scotland.

Alison Blackwell (BSc, MSc, PhD, FRES) is an entomologist best known for her work on biting midges in Scotland. She is author of over 60 original research papers and contributor to several books. She is currently an Honorary Fellow at the University of Edinburgh, from where she runs her own company developing solutions to a whole range of insect problems. As a pet owner and outdoor enthusiast, ticks are never far from her thoughts...

TICKS
YOUR PETS, YOUR FAMILY AND YOU

George Hendry, Darrel Ho-Yen and
Alison Blackwell

mercatpress
www.mercatpress.com

First published in 1998 by Mercat Press
This second edition published in 2006 by Mercat Press
10 Coates Crescent, Edinburgh EH3 7AL
www.mercatpress.com

© George Hendry and Darrel Ho-Yen 1998 and 2006, Alison
Blackwell 2006

ISBN-13: 978-1-84183-084-4
ISBN-10: 1-84183-084-4

CONTENTS

How to remove a tick: 🕷
p. 83

ILLUSTRATIONS and FIGURES

ACKNOWLEDGEMENTS

The authors wish to acknowledge the help of Dr Paul Hillyard, (Natural History Museum, London), Professor Pat Nuttall and Dot Carey (Institute of Virology and Environmental Microbiology, Oxford), Dr Gerhard Soja (Forschungszentrum Seibersdorf, Austria), Kristine MacKenzie and Chris MacKenzie (respectively Ross-shire crofter and keeper), Edmund O'Brien and Mervin Roberts (Selectmen of Old Lyme, Connecticut), Dr Jim Douglas (Fort William), Alan McGinley, Kim Cahill and Debbie Gilham (Raigmore Hospital NHS Trust), Neil MacCrindle for many updates, and the forbearance of Tom Johnstone of Mercat Press. *Tha sinn fada 'nad chomain.*

PREAMBLE

There is a widely held expectation today that the countryside should be a safe and healthy environment for work or recreation. The reality, however, is that, throughout rural Britain, West, North and Central Europe, ticks are present in significant numbers and they carry diseases. One of these, Lyme disease, has attracted wide publicity in Britain, in western Europe and north America in recent years. The result of this publicity is that for some people an innocent day of countryside recreation can be marred by considerable apprehension on finding a tick quietly feeding away on the skin. For others more familiar with ticks, the repeated warnings of the past decade should not go unheeded. Ticks are a potential hazard to humans and animals and should never be ignored.

There are, today, numerous websites dealing with ticks and disease. Unfortunately, the overwhelming majority are written for the very different cultural, biological, medical and environmental conditions prevailing in the United States. European ticks and European tick-borne diseases are very different!

In this book we aim to provide authoritative, plain-language, practical information on European ticks and tick-borne diseases and how to avoid them. The book is written for the hill walker, climber, shooter, fisher, farmer, crofter and forester as well as for all who seek no more than a healthy and rewarding day out in the countryside. For this updated second edition, the original authors are joined by Dr Alison Blackwell who brings her own specialisms in animal health and invertebrate pathology to focus on ticks and tick-borne diseases in livestock and household pets. Each chapter has a quick-read, boxed summary with, at the end of the book, an appendix giving details of every species of tick resident in Britain, and a short bibliography for those who seek more information.

At the end of the day, probably the most effective and sustainable way to combat ticks is through education, and if the reader can put down this book feeling more informed, relaxed but watchful, then we will have achieved our aim.

I
TICKS AND DISEASE
A SHORT GUIDE

Ticks—the Background

- Ticks carry several diseases afflicting livestock, wildlife and humans.

- Lyme disease is one of the major tick-borne diseases of humans.

- Lyme disease is present in Britain, throughout Europe and north America.

- In Britain, the micro-organism causing Lyme disease is carried by our most widespread tick—the sheep tick.

- The sheep tick, despite its name, feeds on deer, cattle, sheep and many smaller mammals in forests, woodland, damp pastures and moorland.

- Lyme disease can be eminently treatable.

The story of tick-borne diseases is a world-wide one of misery and economic devastation to many millions of people drawing their living from the land. For most western Europeans, particularly city dwellers, the story would have remained a tale of misfortune for farmers, a disease of foreign countries. That is until the advent of Lyme disease, the one tick-borne disease which has made headline news in western Europe and north America in recent years.

But the story of tick-borne diseases is much, much older, and in most parts of the world Lyme disease is unknown. Instead, in most regions ticks are known as blood-sucking parasites that carry a wide range of diseases—diseases that afflict Man, his livestock, his domestic pets and wildlife. Globally, ticks rank as one of the most important biological limits to Man's economic activities.

Ticks and disease—a global perspective

Tick-borne diseases have been recognized for centuries and have brought untold misery and economic disaster to many parts of the world. In Britain, Scottish farmers have long suffered the devastations of louping-ill. Two hundred years ago, the Ettrick shepherd James Hogg knew this as thwarter-ill, trembling-ill or louping evil. Once thought of as a tick-borne disease peculiar to the damp pastures of Scotland it is now known from the hill country of England, Wales and from various parts of coastal Europe. Apart from destroying flocks, it afflicts humans, particularly farmers, shepherds, vets and abattoir workers.

And long before louping-ill, a disease known today as haemorrhagic fever had been recorded in Tadzhikistan from the twelfth century. In 1944 this fever spread rapidly westwards into war-torn Ukraine, probably on ticks feeding on the backs of hares. Characterized by fever and bleeding, the disease has now been recorded in Africa, Pakistan and, more recently, in southern Europe. For all his might in war, Man's capacity for belligerence has literally been brought to a halt by ticks. At times the civil war in Zimbabwe in the 1970s had to be suspended following severe outbreaks among the combatants of Mediterranean spotted fever. Today, this tick-borne disease is endemic to southern Europe, much of Africa and

India. War also saw the spread of another tick-borne disease into southern Europe in 1940. Known at the time as Balkan gripe, and today as Q-fever, it is an occupational hazard to sheep farmers, sheep shearers and to meat handlers, leading to fever, pneumonia and hepatitis if untreated. Today, it is present throughout much of Europe.

Another import is African swine fever. First recorded in Kenya before the first World War, farmers there faced a cata-strophic wipe-out of pigs. This tick-borne virus has since spread to Spain, Portugal, France and Belgium. In Italy 100,000 pigs died or had to be slaughtered in 1967. In Malta the disease was only eradicated after the entire pig population had been destroyed. In eastern and central Europe, tick-borne encephalitis has been commonly reported in recent decades. First recognized in Russia in the 1930s, this tick-transmitted viral disease has spread westwards into central Europe and eastwards into Asia, probably with the movement of livestock. In recent years the Austrian health authorities have been suf-ficiently concerned to undertake a programme of mass vaccination of children and adults.

One of the most important livestock diseases in Africa is heartwater, which got its nineteenth century name from the accumulation of fluid round the heart. This tick-borne disease, characterized by fever, twitching, a high-stepping gait and convulsion, is today controlled largely by vaccination of herds. A tick-borne disease widespread in Europe is redwater fever, where the blood of affected cattle becomes thin and watery. Transmitted by our all-too-common sheep tick, outbreaks can be of considerable economic significance.

Wherever large herds are maintained, ticks become a prob-lem. American ranchers in the cowboy era of the mid-nineteenth century witnessed another tick-borne disease, Texas cattle fever, destroy up to 90% of their cattle in susceptible herds. The ranchers themselves, and their families, were afflicted by different tick-borne diseases, Colorado tick fever and Rocky Mountain fever. An outbreak of the latter in Montana in 1899, with severe illness and death among both white settlers and native Americans, was pinned down to a tick carried on dogs. Today, this notifiable disease is widespread in north America, particularly in the east, and, if untreated, can be fatal. It has proved a particular hazard among children playing in woodlands. It took until the early twentieth century to discover that ticks were responsible for transmitting Rocky Mountain fever, Texas cattle fever and Colorado tick fever, and this led to the establishment of the Rocky Mountain Laboratories of the US Public Health Service, as a centre for tick-borne disease research. This was the research centre which was to play a key part in the discovery of the microbe involved in Lyme disease 70 years later.

Lyme disease: 150 years in the making

Two hours out from New York, east on Interstate 95, cross the Connecticut River, take the next exit and drive into another age. This is the world of New England classical timber and brick houses, of sailing ships and sea captains. Here the American impressionists of the early years of the century would meet to paint, and their inspiration still lives. This is the small town of Old Lyme.

Today, as well as painters, the community attracts weekend home-owners and visitors from New York, bird watchers and duck hunters. Five minutes from the town centre visitors congregate at night to watch beavers building dams. Muskrats, coyotes and white-tailed deer are only minutes away. While the human environment is under the guardianship of the Lyme Historic Society, the Old Lyme Conservation Trust cares for the surrounding water meadows, marshes, beaches and woodlands. A New England idyll.

The idyll was shattered in November 1975. In the previous three summers, a dozen children from the small communities of 5000 souls around Lyme had been diagnosed as having juvenile rheumatoid arthritis. Two concerned mothers, Polly Murray and Judith Mensch, could not accept the diagnosis of arthritis in child after child, up and down their roads. They went to the state health authority. Within days of their visit, new reports of arthritis were noted among other children, and several adults, in the three neighbouring townships of Lyme, Old Lyme and East Haddam. Alerted by these reports, the health authorities, at nearby Yale University School of Medicine and led by Dr Allen Steere, tracked down 39 children, the youngest aged 2 years, and a dozen adults, who had recently suffered several painful bouts of swelling in the knee and other joints. The attacks often persisted for only a week or two but recurred at intervals over the following months or years. Several of the attacks of arthritis had begun in the summer of 1972. The affected children were largely from the 5 to 14 year age group, with rather more boys than girls.

The symptoms, however, did not quite fit the classical description of juvenile rheumatoid arthritis. An odd coincidence also emerged. Many patients recalled that the arthritis was preceded by a large red mark or rash on their skin which expanded in size over subsequent days. Physicians, parents and children alike put this down to an insect bite. The next clue came from maps drawn up showing the location of the houses lived in by the affected children and adults. Most houses were close to heavily wooded areas, abounding in white-tailed deer, and located on just four country roads and not in town or village centres. One in every 10 children from this rural backwater had the illness. The children attended two schools, one in Old Lyme, the other 12 miles away in East Haddam. No common exposure such as an immunization programme, a shared swimming pool or a common food source could be traced. More puzzling, perhaps, the onset of the illness occurred in different years in the same families, usually starting in the summer or early autumn.

Because some forms of arthritis are known to occur after infections, rubella and parvovirus especially, most of the patients were tested for a battery of viruses and bacteria. None showed any common pattern of infection. The possibility of a mosquito-borne virus was checked. All tests were negative. By the end of the intensive study of the original 51 patients, the summer of 1976 brought forward 38 new patients. With a total of 89 cases, the authorities needed to give it a simple description—and so the name Lyme disease was born.

Going back to the possibility of an insect bite, with a characteristic large and expanding red mark, the clinicians noted similar reports of such marks in the European medical literature, from Sweden, France and Germany, dating way back at least as far as 1913. This red mark had been long known as *Erythema chronicum migrans* (ECM), medical Latin for an expanding or migrating red mark or ring on the surface of the skin. Some of these European reports linked ECM to the bite of the sheep tick, a creature not found in Connecticut. Nevertheless, the Yale rheumatologists collected 62 populations of American species of ticks from the local community, but these too were negative in the tests. By the early 1980s, whatever it was that might link ECM in Europe and Lyme disease in Connecticut remained elusive.

The key to the mystery lay in publications 60 or 70 years earlier by three dermatologists working independently in different parts of Europe: Alfred Buchwald in Breslau (now

Wroclaw, Poland), Arvid Afzelius in Sweden and Benjamin Lipschutz in Vienna. Between them they had described skin infections characterized as an expanding ring-like rash. Buchwald noted his first observations in 1883, Afzelius his in 1909 and Lipschutz in 1923, such was the pace of research. Because of the superficial similarities with syphylis, some of these records were actually published in journals primarily concerned with venereal disease. By 1921 Afzelius had speculated that the rash might be associated with a tick. Lipschutz went further and noted 'perhaps we are dealing with a skin infection caused through the bite of a tick. Therefore, attention should be directed towards microscopic and bacteriologic investigation of the intestinal tract and of the salivary gland of the tick'. Unfortunately, if Lipschutz himself did follow this up he seems not to have published his findings before his death eight years later. Had the link between ECM and ticks been established firmly, the children of Old Lyme and East Haddam could have been given antibiotic treatment, without ever going on to develop arthritis.

With hindsight, what became known as Lyme disease in the USA in the late 1970s had been there in the European medical records for the best part of a century. Buchwald's description of characteristic skin lesion, which we know to-day from some Lyme disease patients, was described in 1883 in a 36-year-old man. That patient had had the lesion for 16 years—pushing the disease back to 1867. The immediate interest in the skin lesion at that time was in its superficial resemblance to syphilis—itself a serious concern in the pre-antibiotic age. But once the reports of the lesion and rash had got into the medical literature, the pace began to quicken. By 1910, 134 patients in Austria had been described with what was very likely to have been what we know today as Lyme disease. But, apart from the odd report of skin complaints among recent European immigrants, it was unrecorded in the United States.

During the 1920s Swedish, French, German and Austrian physicians began to link the red rash—ECM—with other features of Lyme disease and—an important point—some patients recalled an earlier incident of being bitten by a tick. But still no progress had been made on the cause—was it a virus, bacterium or possibly other toxic material carried by ticks? By the late 1940s several hundred cases of what was to be eventually called Lyme disease had been described in western Europe, and which now firmly linked ECM with a number of muscular and neurological disorders—these often persisting only for several weeks but then, after months or years of apparent recovery, recurring in some patients as rheumatic disease, or forms of meningitis or heart disorders. On questioning, many patients could recall an earlier tick bite. By the early 1960s, German and Czech physicians, now with many hundreds of cases to work from, demonstrated that the incidence of ECM-related disorders overlapped with the geographical distribution of the sheep tick in Europe.

While the Europeans were linking ECM with ticks, four thousand miles away in the summer of 1969, a young physician was bitten by a tick while hunting grouse in Wisconsin. By good fortune he was treated by a colleague familiar with ECM in Europe and within days he became the first diagnosed case of ECM in north America. Meanwhile, back in Old Lyme, Polly Murray had begun to notice an increase in unexplained ailments among her neighbourhood children. A case of ECM was reported from north California, then in 1975 a cluster of three, then four more, cases appeared in south-east Connecticut. Further up the coast the good townsfolk of Old Lyme were, unknowingly, about to make the name of their small town known world-wide.

Six years on and the story now moves off-shore. Opposite Old Lyme lies Long Island. Here, in the summer of 1981, the Swiss-American Willi Burgdorfer was down on his knees hunting for ticks involved in a different tick-borne disease—a spotted fever. He was unsuccessful. However, a colleague gave him some deer ticks from Shelter Island, 18 miles due south of Old Lyme and by then an established area of Lyme disease. Two ticks out of 44 showed poorly stained clumps of irregularly coiled bacteria known as spirochetes. With help from the Rocky Mountain Laboratories, the research centre for tick diseases, the spirochetes extracted from the ticks were successfully cultured. Blood samples from people resident on Shelter Island showed that some carried antibodies to this spirochete, developed following tick bites. And by extraordinary coincidence, the American spirochetes resembled those previously found by Dr Burgdorfer three years earlier in western Switzerland, a known hot-spot for European ECM. Within 12 months of Willi Burgdorfer's discovery, the spirochete was identified in ECM patients in Germany and shortly after in European sheep ticks.

The spirochete was named *Borrelia burgdorferi* in honour of Willi Burgdorfer and proved to be closely related to a number of other borrelias, all of which are carried by ticks, the majority causing a group of diseases called relapsing fevers.

The final piece of the puzzle was to find out from where the American ticks had acquired the spirochete. As ticks live on blood they had most probably acquired the spirochete when feeding on a mammal host. The question was, which mammal? Within three years, the spirochete had been found in field mice in Europe and the white-footed mouse in Connecticut and subsequently in deer and in many other wild and domesticated animals on both sides of the Atlantic. The pieces of the puzzle were all there: the spirochete microbe, the mammalian host as the source of the spirochete, the tick as the transmitter between mouse or deer and human and finally Lyme disease itself.

Lyme disease today

In all probability, Lyme disease has been present in Europe for centuries, largely unrecognized as such. Why the disease appears to have spread so rapidly in New England is less certain; how much is a real geographical spread of the disease and how much is due to increased public awareness is not known. Western Europe and north America have seen a considerable expansion in rural recreation in recent years— camping, rambling, hill-walking, game-hunting and fishing, with many more people exposed to ticks during periods of recreation. Changes in land-use with abandoned pasture reverting to woodland, particularly in New England, have brought deer and deer ticks closer to human habitation. A geographic spread of the spirochete within deer and other wild mammals is a real possibility, certainly within the United States and probably in parts of western Europe, particularly where the deer population has increased. Speculation that the spirochete from Europe might have been imported to North America and beyond in recent decades is not borne out by solid evidence so far—indeed, the North American spirochete shows distinct differences from its European counterpart both in molecular genetic make-up and in the form the disease it causes in humans. Currently, eleven genetically distinct forms of the *Borrelia burgdorferi* spirochete have been described and each one named. The distinction between the different genospecies lies in their ecological preferences, in their different preferred hosts, in their structure (visible under electron microscopes), in their molecular make-up and importantly in the different forms or expressions of Lyme disease. Europe has six of the eleven genotypes, three of which are associated with the European form of Lyme disease. North America has up to five genotypes, most with significant differences to the European forms. The distinctions are important. As a generalisation, North American forms of Lyme disease differ, clinically, from those broadly found in western Europe, though there are some aspects of overlap. Our understanding of the subject of Lyme disease and the different genotypes has become further clouded by the realisation that one tick may pass on more than one disease-causing microbe simultaneously, partly explaining perhaps why some patients develop different symptoms and require different treatments.

Wherever the spirochete, of whatever type, came from, by 1988 Lyme disease had become the most common animal-borne infection of humans in the United States with some 23,000 new cases reported in 2002 alone, up from 12,000 cases in 1995. In just 10 years from the mid-70s Lyme disease had been recorded in 47 states in America, though largely focused on just eight states. In Europe several thousand cases are reported each summer from every country, in north, western and central Europe, as far north as the Novosibirsk region of Russia with smaller numbers in the Mediterranean countries, extending recently across the sea to Morocco. The incidence of the spirochete in sheep ticks also appears to be rising in certain parts of Europe. By 2004 for example, one region of western Germany has recorded increases over a ten-year period.

Lyme disease in Britain

In Britain, a survey conducted by the Institute of Virology at Oxford found that one-third of ticks collected from 230 sites in rural Britain proved positive in tests for the spirochete causing Lyme disease. The survey is incomplete and, indeed, has a bias towards Scotland and certain forested areas of England, probably reflecting more extensive sampling in these areas. Although there have been questions over the reliability and sensitivity of the laboratory test used to detect the spirochete, the important point, however, is that this and other surveys show that the spirochete causing Lyme disease is far more widespread in Britain than previously recognised and, from the experience in other countries, it is here to stay.

Many species of wild animals appear to support spirochete-infested ticks in Britain. In a survey of red and roe deer from 27 sites in Scotland, Wales and England, the spirochete was found in at least one tick from every site. Not surprisingly, people working in deer territory are at risk of acquiring the spirochete following a tick bite. A 1990 survey of field staff from the Red Deer Commission, Forestry Commission and the then Nature Conservancy Council showed that 25% of workers had antibodies to the spirochete. A review of Scottish Natural Heritage field workers found that 26% of those working on the west coast island of Rum, with its then large red deer population, carried antibodies to the spirochete, twice that of their colleagues working on the east coast. In England, 20% of forest workers in Thetford and 29% of New Forest Rangers gave positive reactions in tests. While there may be some problems with false positives in these tests, they do confirm that Lyme disease can be a significant occupational hazard. And not just an *occupational* hazard—in the same New Forest of southern England, one in ten human residents in a localized survey carried antibodies to the spirochete, against one in 50 in a control group of city-dwellers. But city-dwellers are also at risk—screening of urban park workers in Richmond and Bushey Parks in London, each with a large deer population, showed that 16 out of 44 park workers had high spirochete antibody counts. Today, tick-borne diseases in Britain no longer consist only of curiously named diseases like louping-ill of the northern hills; the spirochetes causing Lyme disease are widespread throughout the island.

Lyme disease—the American legacy

Old Lyme, Connecticut, may have given its name to a disease widespread in north America and Europe, but it has also generated a great deal of research and health care in its name. In Connecticut today, the Lyme Disease Foundation and state-based drug companies distribute information warning of Lyme disease. Through web-sites, radio, television and newspapers, efforts are made each year to promote public awareness of ticks and of tick-borne diseases. Numerous plain-language web pages are available originating both in the United States and in Europe with advice on personal protection and on how to spot the symptoms of Lyme disease. Common sense and a sense of proportion may be required, however, to filter out some of the more extreme advice and assertions that plague some of the web-sites. There is, however, some real progress in spreading publicly-available information about the disease.

In just thirty years we have moved from bacteriologists scrabbling among the undergrowth on Atlantic coast North American islands looking for ticks, and zoologists combing the hairs on mice, rabbits, dogs through to deer, and physicians shaking their heads in sympathy over yet another case of juvenile arthritis. Today, most general practitioners have become aware of the disease and, with greatly improved laboratory detection methods for Lyme disease, they can offer effective treatment with a range of antibiotics, particularly when the symptoms are reported early. This, then, is the lasting legacy of Polly Murray's action, thirty years ago in Old Lyme. We Europeans are among the beneficiaries.

2
KNOW YOUR ENEMY

Tick Facts

- All ticks obtain their food by sucking the blood of mammals, birds or reptiles.

- Hungry ticks cling on to the tops of grasses and shrubs ready to ambush their hosts (e.g. walkers with bare arms or legs) as they go by.

- Ticks vary greatly in size—from smaller than a pin-head to the size of a small drawing pin and in colour from black to brown, grey or dark golden-red.

- Ticks carry a greater range of diseases than any other invertebrate pest.

- Ticks acquire and transmit disease-causing micro-organisms during feeding on mammals, birds and reptiles.

- People most at risk from tick-borne diseases include farmers, dairymen, crofters, shepherds and sheep shearers, stalkers, gamekeepers, livestock transporters, abattoir workers, foresters, fencing contractors, countryside rangers, naturalists and ecologists.

- Recreations at risk include countryside walking, hill walking, angling, shooting, bird-watching, camping and caravanning.

- In Britain, ticks bite humans from early spring to autumn; left undisturbed, ticks feed for several days.

- When not feeding, ticks shelter in vegetation where they may survive for a year or more without food.

What are ticks?

Ticks are related to spiders, scorpions, mites and harvestmen (daddy-long-legs). Unlike insects, adult ticks have eight legs, don't fly and lack antennae. All ticks, without exception, are blood-sucking parasites, giving nothing beneficial back to their hosts. And very successful parasites they are too.

Ticks have been known to Man from earliest records. Over 2000 years ago Aristotle catalogued the sheep tick as a 'disgusting parasitic animal'. And the sheep tick, from archaeological evidence, seems to have been an early immigrant to Iceland accompanying the first European settlers. While the Saxons seem to have had only one (polite) word for ticks, *ticca*, the Scottish Gaels evolved many more—*gartan, mial-caorach, sar, sealan, seileann, uamhag,* reflecting perhaps their greater familiarity with tick-infested livestock.

Today we know that, world-wide, the number and range of diseases carried by ticks probably exceed that of all other invertebrates. Ticks carry disease-causing micro-organisms (viruses, bacteria or minute worms) picked up during feeding on one host and subsequently transmitted during feeding to a second host. Once the microbe enters the host's blood stream, other ticks feeding on the same host may themselves become infected. In this way, in many tick-borne diseases, the host, usually a mammal or bird, becomes the reservoir of infection while the tick acts as the transmitter of the disease. In other cases the micro-organism may pass from one generation of ticks to another through its fertilized eggs, the tick serving both as the reservoir and transmitter. In the case of Lyme disease, the most important reservoirs are believed to be small mammals, on which ticks feed early in their life. In Britain, mice, voles, squirrels, hedgehogs, feral cats and birds serve to support the young ticks and carry the disease-causing micro-organism thereafter. Reservoirs for adult ticks and nymphs include sheep, cattle, deer and goats, horses, cats, a number of birds including pheasants, blackbirds and seabirds. Dogs, foxes and rabbits, however, may be less important as reservoirs than previously thought. Whatever the reservoir, the important point is that it is the tick which transmits the disease from host to host.

Ticks most likely evolved alongside land animals about 400 million years ago and today infest almost all mammals, birds, reptiles and amphibians. Fossil ticks have been found in amber dated from 90 million years ago, of a type associated with sea birds. Ticks certainly infested the dinosaurs until those reptiles became extinct 70 million years ago. By then some ticks had adapted to furry mammals by evolving spurs at the top of their legs, the better to grip hairy bodies. Ticks found on the fossilized remains of a woolly rhino, two million years ago, are indistinguishable from tick species present today. Today about 850 species of tick have been described world-wide, so far. They fall into two major groups, hard ticks and soft ticks. Some 22 species have been recorded in Britain (see the *Appendix*) with 12 in Scotland. However, what Scotland lacks in variety, it makes up for in numbers—where one species, the sheep tick (*Ixodes ricinus*) is abundant in the extensive tracts of damp hill pastures and moorlands.

Ticks are not, however, just a countryside hazard. The hedgehog tick (*Ixodes hexagonus*) became a pest of underground air-raid shelters in London during World War II. The passerine tick (*Ixodes frontalis*) infests many birds in city parks and gardens, while the pigeon tick (*Argas reflexus*) has been long established in Canterbury Cathedral. A Scots tick of pigeons, *Ixodes caledonicus*, was first discovered in the (former) coal-mining and iron-foundry town of Denny, Stirlingshire. In contrast, the territory of the seabird tick (*Ixodes uriae*) extends from St Kilda to the Bass Rock, Shetland to the Isle of Wight. However, the species most likely to be met in rural Britain, and indeed throughout western and central Europe, is the sheep tick (*Ixodes ricinus*). As it is also the main vector for Lyme disease in Europe, the account which follows refers largely to this species. Other species differ in the detail.

What does a tick look like?

To first-time observers the outstanding feature of the sheep tick is its extreme range of size (Figure 2.1). After hatching from the egg, the larva has just six legs and is smaller than a pin head, more like a fleck of soot. The next stage towards maturity, the nymph, has eight legs and is about the size of a pin head and it is the nymph that is most frequently met with by humans. The mature adult female, less common on humans, also eight-legged, is about 3 to 4 mm in diameter before feeding, but in her fully engorged state she may expand to 10 mm, the size, shape and colour of a flattened raisin (Figure 2.2).

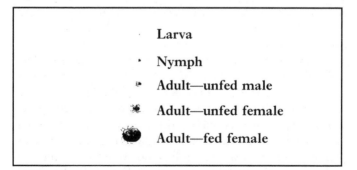

Figure 2.1: The approximate size of the sheep tick *Ixodes ricinus* in its different developmental stages. The nymph is the form most frequently encountered biting humans

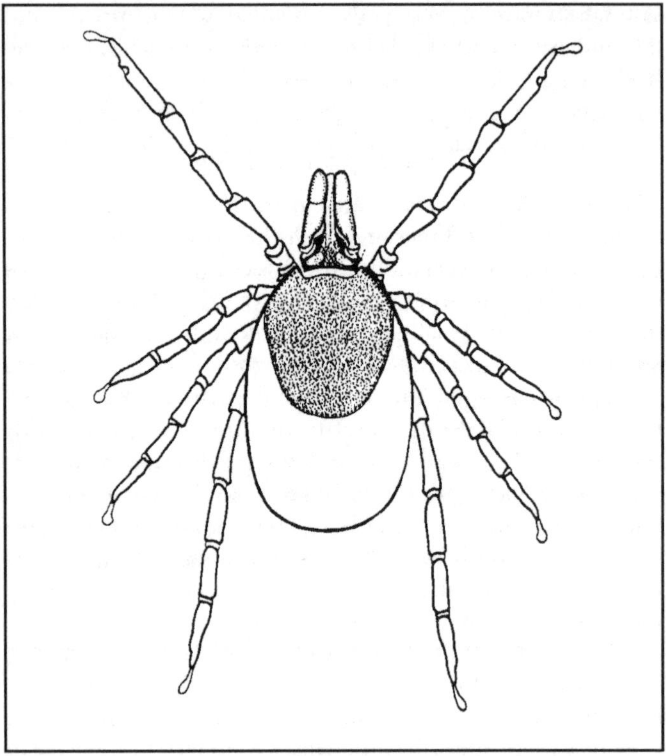

Figure 2.2: A drawing of a female adult sheep tick enlarged about 15-fold (adapted from Hillyard, 1996)

Ticks appear to the eye to be all of one piece, consisting of a flattened oval-shaped black, brown, sometimes grey-brown or dark golden-red body. When feeding the pointed end is buried firmly into the skin of its host, the back end stuck up in the air. Closer examination with a magnifying glass will reveal its walking legs poking out at the side. If there is any doubt, the rule is that if you find a small black spot on your skin which was not there yesterday and does not readily brush off, and particularly if the skin around it is reddish, it is a tick!

Tick biting and feeding

The tick year in Britain starts in early spring, with larvae, nymphs and adults emerging from their over-wintering resting sites deep in vegetation and crevices in the soil, triggered by increasing day length and temperature. The ticks begin their new season, usually in damp weather, by climbing to the top of grasses, bracken, heather and small shrubs. There they adopt their host-searching or questing position. When questing for a host, the tick clings to the top of its plant gently waving its front pair of legs. On these legs it has exceptionally sensitive sensors interpreting small changes in temperature, humidity, odours, particularly carbon dioxide, as well as airborne vibration. Sheep ticks lack eyes, though they appear to respond to passing shadows. These sensors function to detect the presence of potential hosts.

Once alerted to the presence of passing animals, or human legs or clothing, they move fast. Once on the skin of an animal they can travel six inches (15 cm) in ten seconds on a smooth surface. In order to attach themselves to their hosts, ticks first use their leg spurs to grip on to hair or clothing. On humans they will seek out soft spots, behind the knee, in the groin, tummy button, armpits, crook of the arm, neck or the comparative safety of the head. On other mammals and birds, ticks tend to congregate round the head and neck, in areas where the host finds it difficult to lick, scratch or peck.

Ticks talk to other ticks, using not sound but a chemical language. Pheromones—information-bearing chemicals—are used to pass on information about food gathering, assembly, mating, regulation of social organization and host finding. Much research has focused on these pheromones and how they are sensed, because this may be one way to control the behaviour of ticks.

Once it is on board its host and a suitable site has been established, the tick pushes its head down, back end up at a sharp angle, and bites. The minute head comes complete with a pair of articulated sharply-toothed skin cutters. The cutters are coupled to sensors which provide information on both the force required to cut through skin and on the composition of the blood. Once the cut has been opened up, the tick thrusts its barbed headpiece, or hypostome, into the wound to serve as an anchor. Within minutes the tick secretes a rubbery glue, which later cements the head tightly to the skin, making the tick difficult to dislodge.

Ticks seek food by ripping and tearing through the skin layers into the blood vessels. There they suck up the fluids that exude from the wound using their powerful pharynx. Ticks, particularly sheep ticks, are, however, slow feeders taking several days to complete a meal. Only in the final day of feeding are large quantities of blood taken up—what has been called 'the big sip'—during which the tick, particularly the female adult, expands enormously. To enjoy an uninterrupted flow of blood the tick needs to keep the wound open and to suppress the immune response of its host. It does this by incorporating into its saliva a cocktail of potent pharmaceuticals which are pumped into the wound. It is precisely this saliva which can contain infectious micro-organisms and which makse ticks such important transmitters of disease.

Successful feeding over several days is a hazardous time for the tick, not least because of the need to overcome the host's natural blood-clotting response to a wound. The tick does this by injecting through its mouth parts powerful drugs which prevent blood clotting and further suppress constriction of the damaged blood vessels, as well as inhibiting the host's other immune defences. Anti-inflammatory chemicals in the tick saliva also reduce the host's awareness of the tick. Indeed, most humans are not aware that they are being bitten. At best a gentle tickling sensation may develop some hours after attachment. Left undisturbed, the young larval and nymph stages feed for 2 to 6 days. The adult female, however, needs at least a week to complete her feeding, during which she will consume up to 100 times her body-weight in blood. Either before or during feeding she will be mated, just once, by a male roving on the same host. The mating process is complex and appears to involve a distinct ritual. When fully fed the female tick detaches itself from the host, the larvae and nymphs shelter in the vegetation and there moult, while the pregnant adult female seeks shelter near to the soil surface to lay her eggs before finally expiring. The males, meanwhile, may stay on the host searching for further females, sustained by sporadic short blood meals.

No blood-sucking insect can match ticks during feeding. A fully engorged female tick may have consumed 4 to 5 mls of blood over several years. Mosquitoes, clegs and midges take less than 1000th of a ml over a few weeks, at best. Ticks, in large enough numbers, can and do bleed an animal to death—heavily infected seabirds, young deer calves and lambs particularly.

Blood letting apart, ticks can acquire, carry and transmit a wide range of viruses, bacteria, fungi, protozoa and nematodes. No insect transmits such a variety of infections. Unlike almost all bloodsucking invertebrates, ticks can store their blood meal in their intestine often for months without digesting it, making this a favourable environment for the survival of pathogenic organisms.

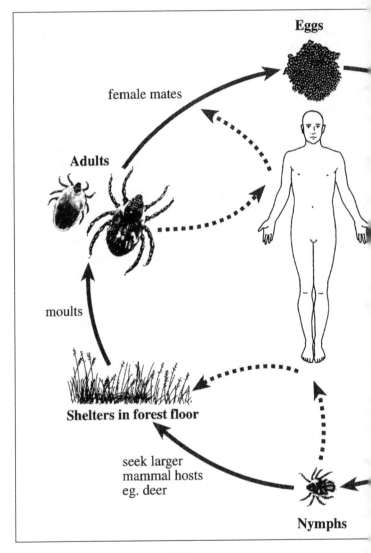

Eggs

female mates

Adults

moults

Shelters in forest floor

seek larger
mammal hosts
eg. deer

Nymphs

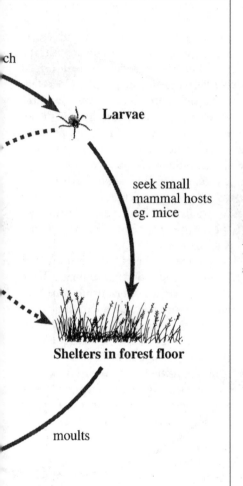

ch

Larvae

seek small
mammal hosts
eg. mice

Shelters in forest floor

moults

Figure 2.3 The life
cycle of the sheep tick
Ixodes ricinus from egg,
to larva, to nymph and
adult. The dotted lines
show opportunistic
feeding on a human.

23

Sheep ticks spend the active part of their two or three years of life searching for and consuming blood meals. The newly hatched larva seeks out small mammals, typically mice, shrews, voles and hedgehogs and, if chance presents itself, the larva will certainly attack humans, particularly bare-legged walkers, bare-armed vets, farmers and shepherds. Once fed, the larva drops off into the vegetation, hides, moults and re-emerges as a nymph, this time to feed, typically, on sheep, young deer, cats, squirrels, birds and, again if chance prevails, on humans. And once again, when replete the nymph drops off its second host, and hides in the vegetation where it moults, this time into the adult sexual stage. The adult, in turn, now searches for larger animals, deer, sheep, cattle. That is the theory. In practice, ticks at all three life stages seem to grab whatever is passing. Sheep, cattle, deer and humans certainly harbour all three forms (Figure 2.3).

Because ticks feed on a range of hosts, they acquire and pass on a range of infectious agents to other animals. They could hardly have been better designed. Once firmly attached, ticks feed slowly, enabling the migration of micro-organisms from the host into the tick or from the tick into host. It is no coincidence that ticks with the widest taste in hosts are usually the most important carriers of infections. Again because they are slow feeders, firmly cemented on to their hosts, ticks are readily transported along with livestock. Ticks and tick-borne diseases are all too easily moved from farm to farm or region to region, while migrating birds will move ticks across continents.

Ticks at rest and reproduction

Ticks are often remarkably long lived, unlike most insects. Some species of soft ticks feeding on seabirds are known to survive for a decade or more. The sheep tick can survive for up to four years in cold areas of the north and two or three years in warmer areas. Their biting activity occurs in two phases, early spring and autumn. In Scotland, north England and Wales, the nymphs and adults engage in host-seeking in April and May when the air temperatures reaches about 7°C. This may be followed by a second round of biting activity in autumn. Further south the biting season starts in February or March, though in colder parts of Scotland seasonal activity may be delayed until June and July. Eggs are laid in mid to late summer and may hatch within a few weeks to give rise to a second bout of biting activity in autumn. Or the eggs may remain as eggs throughout winter. At the end of autumn the tick larvae and nymphs close down all activity and rest over winter, the survivors resuming their quest as hungry individuals the following spring. This ability to close down—called diapause—enables the tick to survive adverse environments and to synchronize development, feeding and reproduction with periods of maximum food availability. After winter, with the return of longer day-lengths and warmer temperatures, the ticks break from diapause and begin the search, or quest, for a blood meal. Successful questing relies on an ambush strategy where the tick climbs the tops of grasses or bracken and clings on with its back legs. The forelegs slowly fold and unfold, gently gathering information on odours, temperature and vibration. When a potential host approaches the tick claws the air more rapidly. If physical contact is made, the now excited tick grasps its host firmly and scuttles up the leg or flank, through hair, fur or under clothing, and within minutes begins the task of feeding. Days later, when fully fed, the tick detaches from its host and drops off into the vegetation to moult or lay eggs. The process of moulting in ticks is gradual and enables any micro-organisms in the tick's gut to be transferred from larva to nymph, nymph to adult, a process which does not occur in many rapidly moulting disease-carrying insects.

A tick, unable to find a host after questing for hours or days, will return to the moist undergrowth to regain body water through surface absorption. Once re-hydrated it climbs up the vegetation to its questing site. Individual ticks have been recorded making this journey up to 20 times in a season. If all else fails and there is no ready meal, the tick may return to diapause and fast for months, even a year. Ticks are long-lived, particularly in cool northern areas, and frequently outlive the lambs and calves on which they initially feed.

The final weeks of life for the mated, fully fed, mature adult female tick is spent laying several thousand, individually waterproofed, eggs, in sheltered damp vegetation or in moist cracks in the soil. During egg-laying the increasingly exhausted female shrivels to half her replete body weight and then expires —a true egg-laying machine converting blood products to new progeny. No blood-sucking insect can match ticks in fecundity.

Where ticks are to be found

Although the sheep tick is well-adapted to living in Man-altered environments, it appears that the favoured ancestral habitat for this species was the deciduous forest. Indeed, on the Continent, the sheep tick is known as the wood tick. Today, in deforested Britain, the sheep tick is abundant on pastures and especially in rough grazings in high rainfall areas of the west. It remains, however, plentiful in woods and plantations throughout Britain. Moorland, hills and forests grazed by deer are often notorious for ticks. And perhaps attracted by walkers, ticks can reach high numbers in the vegetation immediately bordering footpaths.

Figure 2.4: Tick-infested rough grazing in the west Highlands. Note the questing opportunities offered by tall bracken, the shade effects from nearby trees which reduce desiccation and the nearby grazed grassland supporting sheep and deer; altogether an ideal habitat for sheep ticks.

Enormous numbers of ticks can be present in suitable locations. In one forest site in Austria the number of sheep ticks was estimated at about 400,000 per hectare, mostly larvae but with about 90,000 nymphs and 10,000 adults. We have recorded twice this number on short stretches of vegetation flanking footpaths in Scottish hills. Almost certainly, the major limit to tick numbers is drought. Most European ticks are very sensitive to water loss, particularly in periods of warm weather. The sheep tick is adapted to damp conditions and, with a leaky outer skin or cuticle, it is particularly prone to desiccation. Exposure to even short periods of dry conditions forces the tick to abandon questing and to seek refuge in damp soil or vegetation. Sufficiently prolonged dry periods may greatly reduce the tick population. Sheep ticks cannot emulate camel ticks, which survive for considerable periods buried in the sands of the Nile!

The sheep tick, despite its name, feeds on many kinds of wild and domestic animals, and humans too when available. Humans are not, however, the main host, though from a human perspective this may not always seem so. Even though sheep ticks are more likely to feed on livestock, almost any walker in the Highlands and Southern Uplands of Scotland, in Wales, north and south-west England will encounter ticks, particularly nymphs, between April and October. The incidence of sheep ticks may well be less on the cereal-growing drier east coast, but wherever cattle, sheep and deer graze, ticks will be present. Nor will humans be spared if they walk in woodland, almost anywhere in the land. Ticks are a fact of country life—and not just British life. Forests and open countryside walks almost anywhere in France, Germany, Switzerland and Austria will yield as many ticks as in Britain, if not more.

Inevitably, certain occupations are particularly at risk from tick bites, sheep shearing perhaps more than most. Sheep ticks regularly bite farmers, crofters, dairymen and shepherds. Vets, deer stalkers, gamekeepers, livestock transport drivers and abattoir workers are all too familiar with ticks. Even those not involved in handling animals can expect to be bitten— most particularly foresters, fencing contractors, countryside rangers, roadmen, electricity and telephone linesmen, footpath construction gangs and professional ecologists working in rural areas. Most of these folk are familiar with ticks and know what to do when they see an immobile black spot fastened on to their skin!

It is the unsuspecting visitors to the country who may be surprised by ticks—particularly in this age of high expectations of carefree, healthy, rural holidays. The reality is that campers, caravaners, ramblers, climbers, hill walkers, bird watchers, anglers and game shooters must expect to be bitten by ticks, almost anywhere in rural Britain. Their opposite numbers in Connecticut and elsewhere in north America have been well primed for the past twenty years by health education campaigns to look for and to remove ticks promptly. This book attempts to do just that on this side of the Atlantic!

3
INFECTIONS FROM TICKS

Approach to tick infections

- Risks of infection need to be understood.
- All risks are not equal.
- All infections are not the same.
- Travel abroad involves a greater exposure to infections.
- Risks of infection may be reduced by sensible behaviour.
- Risks of infection need to be balanced against the pleasure of the activity.

After a tick bite, an individual may develop many infections. Similarly, if one buys a lottery ticket, it is possible to win several prizes. However, for the vast majority of individuals who receive a tick bite (as with most who buy a lottery ticket), the result is that there is no change in their circumstances. Whilst it is easy to understand the lottery, many find it difficult to know why all tick bites do not result in one or more infections. The explanation is in an understanding of the process of transmission of infection from ticks to humans.

Transmission of infection occurs only when several conditions have been satisfied. These mainly involve the habitat, tick and human being. The place where the tick bite occurs is important, as the local environmental conditions may favour tick survival and some infections may thrive in certain places.

The tick cannot transmit an infection if it is not infected; and if infected, it has to be attached to the human long enough to transmit infection. Lastly, some individuals are more susceptible to tick bites: perhaps because of their body odour, body heat, softness of skin, ease of attachment of tick or some other factor. Previous chapters have considered many aspects of the habitat and the tick, however, this chapter will focus on how such factors affect the development of infections. The winning of the lottery is influenced by the odds: the more tickets one buys, the greater the chance of winning. Infections from ticks are also influenced by the odds, but for infections they are usually referred to as 'risks'.

Risks in the habitat

Ticks like particular living conditions (microenvironment) and this plays an important part in determining the distribution of ticks. Humans get bitten when they invade the tick's habitat. If individuals are aware of the tick's preferred microenvironment, it is possible to avoid places with high tick populations. As ticks may have to survive for prolonged periods without a meal, it is critical that the microenvironment is not hostile to the tick. Temperatures must not be extreme and relative humidity is important. Therefore, humans may reduce the risk of tick bites by walking on tops of hills/mountains rather than at the bottom; or walking in short grass/vegetation rather than long grass/scrubland.

Geography is important. For temperate areas of the world, the longer days and raised temperatures encourage ticks to start questing for hosts. In tropical areas, where daylight and temperatures do not vary as much, the stimulus for tick activity may be the change from dry to rainy seasons. Nevertheless, it must be remembered that even during times of peak tick activity, periods of questing may have to be alternated with periods of rehydration. Further, ticks may become dormant (diapause) if weather conditions are particularly adverse; this ability has been particularly useful in extending tick survival. It is no surprise that ticks are able to survive longer without food or water than any other group of arthropods. Throughout the world, tick populations depend on the combination of a favourable microenvironment and the presence of suitable hosts for blood meals. Avoidance of areas with this combination of factors greatly reduces the risk of developing infections.

Ticks are seasonal creatures. The risk of a tick bite varies with the time of year. Unfortunately, different species of ticks have different seasonal behaviour, but usually the pattern is the same for any one place. As always, local people are usually aware of the seasonal behaviour of the local ticks. For the sheep tick, there is high risk during every year: in England and Wales, spring and autumn are the two danger periods with peak tick activity; for Scotland, warmer temperatures are slightly delayed so there tends to be one period with peak tick activity in late spring-early summer.

As the microenvironment is the main consideration, the seasonal peak in spring on exposed, open land may precede sheltered, protected land by several weeks. The converse occurs in autumn. Although general statements can be made about the seasons, it is not the time of year but the microenvironment which is important, so a warm spring may behave like a cold summer. Within the seasonal peak of tick activity, there are also considerable variations in the peaks of the different stages of ticks (larvae, nymphs, adults). Thus, for each place there is a spectrum of increasing risk of tick bites over several months. In Canada, there is the winter tick (*Dermacentor albipictus*) whose peak activity is from November to April.

If someone wants to wander into the tick's habitat at times of peak activity, it is wise to take appropriate precautions to reduce tick bites. In several countries, especially the United States and Canada, the Governments have taken preventative measures to reduce tick populations (Chapter 6). Walkers in these areas can be reassured that the risks of infection are significantly reduced following these measures.

Risks from the tick

Large tick populations in a given place increase the risk of tick bites and the possibility of infection. It can be difficult to estimate the size of the tick population and this varies dependent on the season (Chapter 2). Nevertheless, it can be useful to have some understanding of the relative numbers. In one study there were some 400,000 ticks per hectare with a distribution of 1 adult to every 20 nymphs and 70 larvae. Fortunately, about 90% of those ticks were not actively questing for hosts. The adult tick population is obviously influenced by the microenvironment, but perhaps the most important factor is the size of the small mammal population which supports the nymphal ticks and allows development into adults. It is also the nymphs that may be undetected on the human because of their small size and so are more likely to transmit infection.

The tick population is reduced by many natural predators. In Africa and the Caribbean, 'tick birds' walk along the backs of large cattle eating any obvious ticks. Chickens are able to remove ticks from cattle as well as from the undergrowth; one study showed that each chicken was able to consume 80 ticks per hour. Apart from birds, ants and beetles can consume significant numbers of ticks. Tick numbers may also be reduced if they themselves become parasitized, such as when the chalcid wasp lays its eggs in an engorged tick which subsequently dies as the wasp larvae develop. Thus, areas rich in tick predators are likely to have lower risks of tick bites. These areas tend to be those supporting a rich wildlife (some moorlands and forests) in contrast to heavily managed arable land.

Whereas most tick species feed only on specific hosts, ticks that can transmit infections to humans are able to feed on several hosts. Nevertheless the human is not usually the main or preferred host, but rather a convenient, opportunistic blood meal. Simply, the human is in the wrong place at the wrong time. Once bitten, the time a tick spends on the host will vary: many feed within 2-3 days, but others may take much longer. Humans may make use of this delay in feeding: if ticks are removed within 12 hours of becoming attached, infection is avoided. Even if tick removal is delayed to 48 hours, infection may not occur. The important lesson is to inspect the body after a venture within tick territory.

As a relatively small number of ticks are infected and there may not be many opportunities for new ticks to become infected, it is somewhat surprising that infections are propagated and do not die out. A part of the answer is that many infections invade the ovaries of ticks and so can infect thousands of eggs, each of which on hatching may subsequently pass on the infection. This method of infecting the ovaries is believed to be important in the transmission of infection, especially with infections such as babesiosis. Fortunately, infection of the ovaries is erratic or there would be even more infected ticks. The relative importance of a tick biting an infected host and subsequently transmitting the infection to another host is unknown.

Another method of maintaining infected ticks in a given place is when the infectious organism invades the salivary glands of an immature tick. The result is that subsequent stages of the tick, such as the nymph, can be infectious and transmit disease. If the infection had not established itself in the salivary glands, subsequent stages of the tick might not have been infectious. Thus, infection of the ovaries and salivary glands allow the infectious agent to be maintained in a particular area for several generations of ticks which may span many years. It is thus possible for local people to be aware that certain areas of the countryside are infected by a particular microorganism. Fortunately, only a small number of humans will become infected compared to other animals. Also, these humans would have wandered into tick territory without taking appropriate precautions against becoming infected.

Risks from human behaviour

If humans avoid the habitat of ticks, they will not get bitten

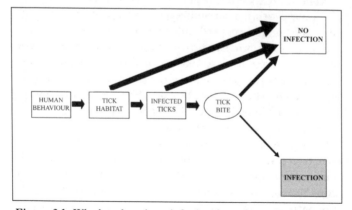

Figure 3.1: Whether there is an infection depends on the interaction of human behaviour, tick habitat, infected ticks and the tick bite. The size of the arrows show that there is mostly no infection.

by a tick, and there will be no risk of infection (Figure 3.1). If they do go to places with a tick population, tick bites can be avoided by simple measures such as total coverage of the body, which is very effective if somewhat uncomfortable. Inevitably, there are compromises for comfort, so only the lower body is usually covered or soap is rubbed on the legs to discourage tick bites.

For ticks to have successful blood meals, they have to overcome the human's body defences against bleeding and foreign material. After an injury, blood vessels contract and the blood clots around the injury to prevent further bleeding. To overcome this defence mechanism, ticks release from their salivary glands several substances which dilate blood vessels and increase blood flow (prostaglandins). Also, the tick injects into the bite substances that stop the human's blood clotting (anticoagulants). Thus, the tick is adept at overcoming human body defences which prevent bleeding.

The human's natural protection against other organisms (immune system) is more difficult to bypass. The tick is most successful with hosts with whom it has associated for hundreds of years. Simply, with time the tick has been able to find ways of by-passing the host's immune system. Thus, some animals can have numerous tick bites without developing immune reactions, for example white-footed mice and the tick *I. dammini*, whereas *I. dammini* can produce a severe immune reaction in meadow voles.

The immune reactions of hosts, including humans, are complex. Two components of the immune system have to be considered: non-specific (applies to any foreign material entering the body) and specific (directed against individual foreign material). With a first exposure to foreign material (for example, saliva from ticks), there are mainly immediate non-specific responses. Initially, there is a non-specific immune response with inflammation (redness, itchiness and swelling of the skin) which interferes with tick feeding. These immediate non-specific responses depend on the actions of several blood cells, but can be reduced by drugs, such as anti-histamines. Over the next 2-3 weeks, animals start to develop several specific protective proteins (antibodies) against the tick saliva. Subsequently, these individuals are regarded as immune and after a second tick bite will produce immediate interaction between these antibodies and tick saliva. There is a specific response with the area of the tick bite becoming filled with watery fluid instead of red blood cells.

The result is that the tick's red blood cell meal is dramatically reduced. Further, this inadequate meal can result in direct damage to the tick and prevent its subsequent development. These mechanisms are useful for animals who have repeated tick bites, whereas animals who rarely have tick bites will not have a vigorous immune reaction and so be at higher risks of infection. Ticks that remain attached to an immune individual feed slowly or not at all and may die as they are unable to feed. In addition the itchiness of the site and prolonged attachment predispose to the tick being removed by scratching by the host. Some deer may have so much blood removed by tick bites that the deer dies without the time to mount an immune response, although the tick-deer relationship is longstanding.

The position of the tick and the human is quite different, as humans are usually accidental hosts for the tick. Yet, it is still noticeable that humans who have frequent contact with ticks often do not have evidence of many tick-borne infections. A likely explanation is that these humans have developed immune reactions to a tick attachment which interfere with feeding. Several substances may initiate the immune reaction to ticks, for example, the cement with which the tick attaches to the host or saliva from the tick. Similarly, in animals that are not frequent hosts for ticks, it requires repeated tick bites before the animal has circulating antibodies which are able to act immediately and reduce tick attachment, feeding and the blood meal. The time of attachment and length of feeding can therefore be influenced by the human's immune system.

Individuals who have developed immunity to tick saliva may be in the best position, as their immune system may interfere with tick attachment and feeding and so prevent the tick passing any infections to these individuals. Those persons who have had a particular infection before may only be immune to developing that same infection again, but be susceptible to tick bites and the development of other infections. As in Figure 3.1, infections can only result in a susceptible human who is in a place with ticks and who gets bitten by an infected tick. In addition, the tick must be attached long enough to transmit infection and the human's immune system must have failed in preventing the infection from being established.

Infections

It is easy to understand that if one does not get a tick bite, or that the tick is not infected, there will be no infection, (Figure 3.1). However, it can be more difficult to understand that an infected tick bite may not result in infection. The problem is in understanding the term 'infectious dose'. Simply, this means that unless there are sufficient infectious organisms transmitted in the tick bite, no infection will result. Small numbers of infectious organisms can be easily destroyed by the human immune system, whereas large numbers are too much for the immune system of susceptible individuals.

Infections transmitted by ticks can be classified into three groups mainly dependent on size: viruses, bacteria and larger organisms. Viruses are very small organisms which are not visible to the human eye without a very powerful microscope; viruses also require to invade living cells before they can multiply. Bacteria are much bigger and do not need living cells to multiply. Larger organisms vary tremendously in their size and complexity and are essentially all of the other infectious organisms apart from viruses and bacteria. In this book, tick infections will be considered in these three groups. However, it should be remembered that the requirements of viruses, bacteria and larger organisms for survival vary enormously. The presence of particularly favourable growing conditions in the tick will allow perpetuation of certain infections.

Humans can be preoccupied with whether or not they develop a particular infection (e.g. Lyme's disease, louping ill). However, the development of any infection is a result of a complex process in which very many factors interact. The attitude of an individual is one in which it should be recognised that many criteria must be fulfilled before one gets infected. The process may be interrupted at several points and therefore one should not worry disproportionately. To return to our lottery analogy, when one buys a lottery ticket it is premature to worry about how one may spend a jackpot of millions of pounds. It is best to worry when you see your winning numbers. Then, if you feel that you might not cope with having millions of pounds, you simply do not claim your prize. One objective of this book is to let you have information so that you know when you should be worried, and what options are available to you at each stage.

4
TICK-BORNE HUMAN DISEASES

Infections from ticks

Infections only arise if:
- the tick's habitat is invaded at the right season.
- the tick is infected.
- the human is susceptible to infection.
- the human receives an 'infectious dose'.

Human disease is the result of a disturbance to normal health and results in an individual developing several complaints (symptoms). This chapter will deal with human disease unless otherwise stated. A tick bite is an injury to the individual. Such events may result in disease in several ways which can be conveniently classified as early (hours and days) and later (days and weeks) effects. There are many precautions which one can take to avoid disease and these will be emphasized in this chapter.

What are early effects of tick bite?

Very many individuals will not have any adverse reactions to the tick bite. Initially, the bite is like a small scratch from a rose bush. Afterwards, the most common result of tick bites is probably local allergic reactions. These are a result of the body's immune system trying to deal with the injury. Various components of the tick, especially saliva, can act as a stimulus to the immune system and the result in an uncomfortable, red, itchy bite. This is probably the most common tick-borne human disease and the condition usually resolves in a few days. In individuals who are allergic (usually with a history of eczema, asthma or hayfever) there can be a more pronounced reaction to the tick bite. This may manifest as a very large area of affected skin, usually with the development of fluid under the skin forming an uncomfortable area similar to a very severe sunburn. Normally, there is complete healing of the skin, but this may take a few more days. At the same time, the patient may develop several uncomfortable symptoms such as malaise (feeling unwell), nausea, dizziness, headaches and muscle pains. In a very small number of individuals, there is a very severe reaction which is described as an anaphylactic shock: this reaction involves the whole body and may result in the individual becoming unconscious, and needing emergency treatment in a hospital.

A local allergic reaction to a tick bite produces mainly itchiness. This can result in the patient, especially young children, vigorously scratching the area. Inevitably, especially with dirty fingernails, such scratching may introduce bacteria into the tick bite. Several bacteria (especially *Staphylococcus aureus* or *Streptococcus pyogenes*) may produce quite severe infections. Even without scratching, the tick bite may become infected. This is because the tick bite produces an area of damaged skin which if rubbed against other objects such as dirty clothes, can result in an infected area. This is especially common in unhygienic living conditions. Fortunately, most of these infections just result in small pustular sores (usually getting better without treatment but occasionally needing antibiotics), and do not have generalised reactions in the body. Occasionally, especially if a large area of skin is involved, the bacterial infections from scratching or clothing will result in serious infection throughout the body and manifest as severe fever, headache, nausea, muscle pains and even unconsciousness. In these individuals, the bacterial infection has been disseminated (spread by the blood), and urgent antibiotic treatment is required.

It is important to be aware that these early effects of tick bites have the potential for development into severe disease. Thus, it is best to remove the tick and then to cover the area with a bandage. This allows the area not to be scratched and also prevents other bacteria getting into the bite.

What are the late effects of tick bite?

The late effects of tick bite are due to toxins and infections. Toxins are introduced into the human body by the tick bite and can produce local or disseminated effects. These toxins are not infectious agents themselves but are material produced by the tick which may produce severe disease. Such toxins are distinct from toxins produced by bacteria (from ticks) multiplying in the human body. Fortunately, not very many ticks are able to produce these toxins and such reactions are very rare in Britain. Tick toxins affect animals much more than humans. Symptoms usually appear some days after the tick bite. These toxic reactions have been described all over the world, but especially in tropical countries such as Africa and Australia. There are a variety of symptoms which animals may develop, such as gnashing of teeth, frothy saliva and trembling. In Africa, sweating sickness is very important as it affects many species of animals. Fortunately, a similar reaction in humans is very rare.

Other late effects are tick-borne human infections. Infective agents (Table 4.1 and 4.2) have been around for a long time and have a complex relationship with their human hosts. Very many infections do not result in any symptoms in humans.

Thus, the human will not know that he/she has been infected unless they have a blood test; such infections are called asymptomatic. The majority of infections probably produce complaints of fever and malaise, often being described as 'flu-like' illnesses. In a minority of infections, there are characteristic symptoms which can identify the infectious agent. The spectrum of symptoms seen with all infections is also present with any one infectious agent. Thus any one infectious agent may result in asymptomatic infection, a flu-like illness or a more characteristic complaint (such as a rash or joint pain).

What are the effects of tick toxins?

Tick paralysis is the most important toxic effect of a tick bite and some 40 species of ticks can produce these toxins. Each year, large numbers of livestock and pets are affected and thousands of animals die as a result of these toxins. Fortunately, humans are very rarely affected and tick paralysis is mainly found in North America and Australia. The condition would probably have to be imported into Britain. There is usually an incubation period of 5–7 days in which there may be symptoms of malaise, nausea and headache. Paralysis of muscles on both sides of the body then follows, usually affecting the lower extremities first and then proceeding up the body. The patient's temperature is usually normal and there are no signs of infection from laboratory tests. When the chest muscles are involved, the patient may die from respiratory failure unless they can be adequately treated in an intensive care unit.

In North America, the main tick vectors are *Dermacentor andersoni* and *Dermacentor variabilis*. Symptoms may progress for up to a week, but normally progression is more rapid. In very young children, there may be raised temperature and a more acute course with death in 1-2 days. In most cases removal of the attached tick(s) prevents further deterioration and the patient starts to recover completely. This is not the case with the Australian tick, *Ixodes holocyclus*, where removal of the tick can result in a sudden deterioration in the patient's condition. It is believed that the trauma of the removal of the dead tick with damage to blood vessels may result in release of more toxins into the blood stream. In these cases it may be better to kill the tick but to leave the dead tick at the site of attachment. Diagnosis is often dependent on a clinician's awareness of the condition. Two important factors are: the clinical picture of the paralysis and the finding of an engorged tick on the body, often as a result of 5-6 days attachment. Sadly, in many cases the condition is not suspected and the tick is only found after death at a post-mortem examination of the body. Fortunately, this is not a common problem in Britain.

What are the effects of tick infections?

Tick infections can be classified into three main groups according to their causative agent: viruses, bacteria and larger organisms. Every country has its own most common human infectious agents for each main group. The main infectious agents in each group for Britain are in Table 4.1. There are many more infectious agents for the rest of the world, but the ones most likely to be imported into Britain (by individuals having tick bites while abroad) are in Table 4.2. In this chapter, the infectious agents which have been described in Britain will be discussed in great detail. Obviously with the ease of jet travel, it is possible for individuals to go on holiday and return with exotic infections to Britain. As these individuals may readily recall a tick bite, the last section of this chapter

Table 4.1 British tick-borne human diseases

Organisms	Disease	Frequency	Clinical Effects	Treatment
VIRUSES				
Flavivirus	Louping ill	*uncommon*	encephalitis	supportive
BACTERIA				
Borrelia burgdorferi	Lyme disease	*common*	fever skin nervous system joints heart	antibiotics
Coxiella burnetti	Q fever	*uncommon*	fever heart lungs nervous system	antibiotics
Ehrlichia phagocytophilia	Ehrlichiosis	*not common*	fever joints lymph nodes	supportive, occasionally antibiotics
Bartonella henselae	Bartonellosis Cat-scratch disease	*not common*	fever lymph nodes nervous system	antibiotics
LARGER ORGANISMS				
Babesia spp	Babesiosis	*uncommon*	fever jaundice anaemia	antibiotics

will briefly discuss the infections in Table 4.2. With all these infections, it is important to remember that infection may not necessarily follow a tick bite or symptoms result from an infection (Chapter 3).

For the infections in this chapter, humans are not an important part of the infectious agent's life cycle. Humans usually get infected because they have wandered into the habitat of the tick. As humans encroach more on forested areas (see Chapter 1), the likelihood of tick bites is increased. In Lyme, for example it was found that new houses which had been built by encroaching on tick-infected areas had high population of ticks on their lawns. The exact frequency of the infections in Table 4.1 is not known. Sadly, there are very few large population studies on tick-borne infectious diseases. Nevertheless, the diseases in Table 4.1 will be discussed in order of their perceived frequency and medical importance.

What is Lyme disease?

This is probably the most important tick-borne infection in Britain. Although there is a greater public and medical awareness of this condition, it is probably still under-recognised.

Occurrence

The occurrence of Lyme disease is related to the distribution and infection in ticks. This world-wide infection is particularly prominent in forested areas in Britain where 5%–10% of the human population may have become infected. Places that are exposed and windy, such as tops of mountains, are too hostile for ticks. Infection usually peaks in the months of June and July. Lyme disease is found in patients of all ages but especially in the most active and those exposed to tick bites. The causative organism is a bacterium called *Borrelia burgdorferi*.

Symptoms

Many patients are asymptomatic and do not know that they have developed the infection. Infection therefore does not

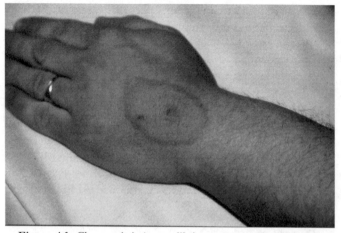

Figure 4.1: Characteristic 'target-like' appearance of an *erythema migrans* rash.

necessarily result in disease. Disease can be classified as early localized, early disseminated or late disseminated. Early localized disease usually follows 3–32 days after a tick bite. A flu-like illness with fever, malaise, muscle pain, joint pain and a sore throat is common. A characteristic rash (called *erythema migrans*) is found in some patients (more in North American patients, less in European patients). This rash starts with a raised, red swelling around the tick bite and gradually expands in all directions, the edges of the rash remain red and inflamed whereas there is central clearing of the rash to produce a characteristic 'target-like' lesion (Figure 4.1).

Early disseminated disease presents with central nervous system involvement: with a headache, stiff neck and photophobia (this triad of symptoms are due to meningitis). Patients may also be confused with reduced concentration and poor memory (usually described as encephalitis). Nerves in the brain (cranial nerves) may be affected and result in facial paralysis (cranial nerve palsies). Involvement of nerves in the rest of the body (peripheral nerves) may result in loss of sensation and tingling of affected areas.

Late disseminated disease can present with:

i) central nervous system involvement weeks or months after the tick bite.

ii) the heart with chest pain and irregular beats.

iii) joints with pain and swelling which can seriously limit mobility.

iv) gastrointestinal tract and result in abdominal pain, tenderness and diarrhoea.

v) liver and spleen, resulting in enlarged organs with tenderness and discomfort.

vi) chronic skin rashes, which are rare and can be difficult to diagnose.

Diagnosis

The diagnosis can be made clinically on the characteristic skin rash. In the absence of this rash, diagnosis is more difficult and relies on a clinician's awareness and laboratory tests. There are a variety of tests that can be done on blood samples to identify infection. It is useful to look for antibodies (produced by the body's immune system) against the infectious organisms. Unfortunately, many of these tests may take 3-6 weeks after infection to become positive. Tests may appear falsely negative early in the illness or with antibiotic treatment and may need to be repeated.

Management

The object of management is to kill the organism, to prevent disease progression and to reduce symptoms. Before treatment is started, there must be an assessment of the clinical situation:

i) the risk of infection depends on the length of infected tick attachment: under 24 hours there is little risk; 48 hours, 50% risk; 72 hours, almost certain infection.

ii) infection occurs in about 10% of people bitten by infected ticks so treatment of all individuals who have been bitten by ticks, is not recommended.

iii) characteristic skin rashes must be treated.

iv) late disseminated disease should be treated, but complete resolution of symptoms may not occur.

v) treatment should be considered in anxious patients who may have infection.

vi) asymptomatic individuals with positive blood tests probably should not be treated.

Treatment

Treatment must be supervised by a medical practitioner. For early disease, several antibiotics are useful (doxycycline, amoxycillin, ceftriaxone or cefotaxime). In patients with penicillin allergies, erythromycin or chlarithromycin may be used. For late disease, oral antibiotics may not be successful and parenternal treatment (given into muscle or blood) may be required.

Prognosis

Despite antibiotic treatment, symptoms recur in 50% of patients although severity and duration are greatly reduced; occasionally recurring symptoms may last several years. Early disease, cranial nerve palsies and meningitis have a good prognosis. Most central nervous system involvement usually has a favourable outcome; only a few have a tendency to chronic or recurrent disease. Joint involvement usually resolves but response may be slow, often needing further treatment. In late disease, recurrence is not usual but can occur. Patients may need careful monitoring for months or years depending on the severity of symptoms.

What is Q fever?

The 'Q' here refers to 'query'. This is because when this illness was first described, no-one knew what was the causative agent. This worldwide, common infection of animals, birds and ticks is now known to be caused by the organism *Coxiella burnetti.*

Occurrence

Infection usually occurs after inhalation of airborne infected particles of bacteria, especially from excreted material from animals, birds and ticks. Consumption of infected, unpasteurised milk is also a source of infection. A common route of infection is from an infected animal after it has given birth when there is a large infected placenta. Infections as a result of a tick bite are very, very rare. Occupations that are particularly at risk are farmers, abattoir workers and vets.

Symptoms

After an incubation period of 2-3 weeks, many patients are asymptomatic and do not know that they have developed the infection. With patients who have symptoms, there is a wide spectrum of disease from a mild fever to very severe illness with neurological or cardiac involvement. Often there is a sudden onset with chills, headache, weakness and severe sweats. There may be a cough as the lungs can be involved, but more importantly there is disturbance in liver function, and infection of the lungs or heart. A very serious long term complication is infection of the valves of the heart and in many cases, without appropriate treatment, the individual may require multiple valve replacement operations. Very rarely there is severe neurological disease.

Diagnosis

The diagnosis is made by looking for antibodies to the organism in a sample of blood. These tests may also be used to monitor management.

Management

Specific antibiotics can be given for the treatment of the infection, usually tetracyclines or chloramphenicol. Such treatment must be prescribed and monitored by a medical practitioner. In individuals with chronic disease, treatment may need to be prolonged. When the heart valves are involved, surgical replacement of these may be required.

Prognosis

Only a very few patients die in the acute phase, usually because they have not been treated. The prognosis is very good for individuals who do not develop heart complaints. For the general public, it is important to avoid drinking unpasteurised milk from cows, goats and sheep. There should also be care when handling tissues such as the placenta from potentially infected animals and other materials (hides, skins and animal by-products).

What is Ehrlichiosis?

This is a common illness in dogs, sheep, horses and cattle. Recently, it has been increasingly recognised in humans. It is probably an infection which is not common in Britain, but as the disease is not easily identified, the diagnosis of 'just a viral infection' is usually made in the cases that occur. The illness is called Sennetsu Fever in Japan.

Occurrence

Although ehrlichiosis is a common, worldwide infection of animals, the numbers of human beings that have been infected are unknown. Most cases occur during the spring and summer. In Britain and most of Europe, *Ixodes ricinus* is the tick most involved in the transmission of this infection. The usual causative agent of this tick-borne infection is *Ehrlichia phagocytophilia*, but other members of this group of bacteria are occasionally involved. In different parts of the world, different ticks and ehrlichia species are involved.

Symptoms

In humans, after an incubation period of 1-3 weeks, an asymptomatic infection usually develops. The most characteristic acute presentation is an illness of sudden onset, high fever, headache and nausea. The patient often has very painful muscles and joints. In about a quarter of patients there is a rash, often a result of bleeding into the skin. Many patients show abnormalities of the bone marrow, with a reduction of white cells (blood cells which especially deal with infection) and platelets (blood components responsible for stopping bleeding). This involvement of the bone marrow is a frequent complication in dogs, and can cause death. Other complaints in animals are extensive weight loss, reduced milk production and, among pregnant animals, abortion is common. However, in both humans and animals, this infection is also more likely to present as a non-specific illness with flu-like symptoms. In many cases, the patient may not be ill enough to warrant blood investigations and the precise diagnosis is never made.

Diagnosis

Diagnosis depends on an awareness of the condition among doctors. The presence of a history of tick bites and exposure during the spring or summer with the characteristic symptoms in a particular area of the country should alert the physician. Laboratory examination of the patient's blood will demonstrate a reduced white cell and platelet population. In addition, microscopic examination of blood samples may actually identify the causative organisms in white cells. Alternatively, patients may have their blood examined by more complicated laboratory tests to detect antibodies to the organism.

Management

Objectives of treatment are to correct the abnormalities in the blood, reduce symptoms and to remove bacteria. Appropriate antibiotic treatment will kill the bacteria, and the drug of choice is tetracycline. Patients may also require replacement of the blood components that are affected, especially to reduce any bleeding. As with other tick-borne infections, prevention of tick bites is an important factor in reducing the number of cases of affected individuals.

What is Babesiosis?

Babesiosis is a very common protozoan infection of animals, but rarely affects humans. Among domestic livestock, especially cattle, there can be a 90% mortality in susceptible herds in the United States of America. Fortunately, the practices of dipping and tick control can dramatically reduce this infection.

Occurrence

Babesiosis shows a similar geographic distribution to Lyme disease, but the epidemic spread of Lyme disease among humans does not appear to occur with Babesiosis. In Britain, most infections are probably transmitted by the tick, *Ixodes ricinus*, while many in the babesia group of bacteria may be involved, it is mainly *Babesia microti* in Britain. In Europe most described cases have been in individuals who have had their spleen removed (a condition described as 'splenectomy'). This is different from North America where both normal individuals and those with splenectomy have been affected. It is likely that all human beings may be susceptible to this infection, but that it can be more severe if an individual has had a splenectomy.

Symptoms

After a 1–4 weeks incubation period, a flu-like illness usually develops. The onset may be acute with extreme fever, malaise, headache, chills, and increased sweating. The infectious agent principally infects red blood cells and this produces destruction of these cells. The position is like malaria and the symptoms are similar. The patient has very black urine due to the haemoglobin from the destroyed red cells, and there can be a resultant anaemia (reduced haemoglobin in the blood). The fever comes and goes but does not have the same pattern as malaria. Like malaria, the parasite can persist for several months, and chronic conditions such as cirrhosis of the liver may develop. Illness may resolve in a few weeks or may last many months or years.

Diagnosis

Blood is usually examined as for malaria, and the diagnosis is made by seeing babesia with a microscope. Unfortunately, this can be difficult when there are few organisms in the blood. Tests may need to be repeated. It may also be useful to look for antibodies.

Treatment

Treatment is usually clindamycin and quinine, but adverse effects of the drugs are common. Recently, atovaquone and azithromycin have been used and appear to cause fewer side effects. Other supportive treatment, especially blood transfusions, may be necessary.

Prognosis

In most cases the individual makes a complete recovery. A few cases are fatal with a rapid progression of disease, especially in those with splenectomy. Occasionally, the illness becomes chronic.

What is Louping ill?

Louping ill disease of animals has been recognised for many centuries. The name comes from the old Scots word 'loup' which was used to described the infection of the brain (encephalitis) effect in sheep which caused them to 'spring into the air'. Although the first human case was described in 1934, the disease seems to be less common in the last decade.

Occurrence

Occurrence of louping ill depends on the presence of ticks which transmit infection. In Britain this is *Ixodes ricinus*. The infection is particularly prevalent in areas where there are many sheep, especially on rough grazing and hill pastures. In Britain this means that it is found in Northern Scotland, the Western Isles, North Wales, North England and in Ireland. Humans who have close association with animals are most likely to be affected. Occupations such as farmers, butchers, abattoir workers, vets and laboratory workers have an increased risk of developing this infection.

Symptoms

After an incubation period of 3-7 days, the infection develops. In most cases it is asymptomatic. In a large number of cases, the symptoms are of a flu-like illness with high fever, headache, malaise, anorexia, dizziness, muscle and joint pain. The most characteristic presentation is of an illness with two phases. The first phase is a fever with flu-like symptoms. Then there is a short period of improvement and the patient feels better. This is followed by the second phase of severe neurological involvement, characterised by high fever, meningitis (severe headache, photophobia and neck stiffness), tremors of the head and limbs, vomiting, and paralysis. The paralysis may be as in poliomyelitis, with severe paralysis, especially of the limbs.

Diagnosis

The diagnosis is usually made by the clinical presentation and the history of a tick bite. Again, an increased awareness of the condition by the physician is critical in making an early diagnosis. Confirmation of the diagnosis is by examination of blood samples for specific antibodies to the louping ill virus. Antibodies may take several weeks to develop and several blood samples may have to be taken.

Management

For most cases, management is of the symptoms and providing support for the patient. In a very few cases, especially when the symptoms involve the nervous system (meningitis, encephalitis, or poliomyelitis-like symptoms) the patient may require admission to hospital. In hospital, the patient can be given support whilst the viral infection runs its course. There is no specific treatment to kill the virus.

Prognosis

Fortunately, the vast majority of patients have a mild illness after which there is complete recovery. In a few individuals, the illness involves the central nervous system and then the recovery may be prolonged. In some cases, convalescence may last years and the patient can suffer recurrence of central nervous system symptoms.

Cat-scratch disease (Bartonellosis)

This is principally a result of cat bites or scratches. However, recently ticks have been shown to transmit the causative organism, *Bartonella henselae*. Infection usually manifests as a flu-like illness, painful lymph nodes or with nervous system involvement. Other organs can be more rarely affected. The diagnosis can be made by antibody tests or biopsy of affected tissues. Treatment is with antibiotics such as tetracyclines, erythromycin or ciprofloxacin.

What are other worldwide viral infections?

Throughout the world there are numerous viral infections which can be transmitted by tick bites. As the list probably runs into hundreds of viral infections, only the important ones will be discussed in this chapter. The main viruses are as in Table 4.2. Nevertheless, it should be remembered that in any one country in the world, their own tick-borne viral infection will be more important. In this chapter, the importance of an infection is its likelihood of being imported into Britain by individuals being infected abroad, either on a short holiday or from working abroad.

Occurrence

Outbreaks of each infection will depend on the tick life cycle. This will be dependent on which part of the world is being visited. In addition, an individual tick may have a different seasonal peak in different countries, dependent on the weather.

Table 4.2 Other worldwide tick-borne human diseases

Organism	Disease	Occurrence	Clinical Features
VIRUSES			
Flavivirus	Tick-borne encephalitis	Europe, Asia	encephalitis paralysis
Flavivirus	Powassan encephalitis	Canada USA, Russia	encephalitis
Flavivirus	Omsk haemorrhagic fever	Russia	bleeding fever
Flavivirus	Kyasanur Forest disease	India	bleeding, fever meningitis encephalitis
Nairovirus	Nairobi sheep disease	Africa, India	fever
Nairovirus	Crimean-Congo haemorrhagic fever	Europe, Africa Asia, Middle East	bleeding fever
Orbivirus	Colorado tick fever	USA, Canada	fever
BACTERIA			
Rickettsia rickettsii	Rocky Mountain spotted fever	North and South America	bleeding fever, rash
Rickettsia conorii	Boutonneuse fever (Mediterranean spotted fever)	Africa, Asia India, Europe	fever, rash
Rickettsia sibirica	North Asian tick typhus	Siberia, Asia Mongolia Eastern Europe	rash, fever
Borrelia recurrentis	Relapsing fever	Asia, Africa South America North America	relapsing fever
Francisella tularensis	Tularaemia	North America Mexico, Europe China, Japan	ulcer, eyes enlarged glands abdomen

As can be seen by Table 4.2, most infections are due to flaviviruses or nairoviruses.

Symptoms

After an incubation period of 1–2 weeks, a number of patients will develop an asymptomatic infection. Of those who develop a symptomatic infection, there are three main clinical presentations:

1. An acute illness involving the central nervous system, with meningitis or encephalitis leading to paralysis, coma and death. Such fatal illnesses are fortunately not common.

2. An acute onset with fever, occasionally with a rash, and less commonly with central nervous system involvement.

3. An acute onset of fever and bleeding (haemorrhagic fever). As bleeding may be internal or external, the patient is seriously ill and fatalities may be high.

Diagnosis

The diagnosis is usually made by the characteristic symptoms in the patient, and an awareness of the infection in the particular area in which the patient has resided or visited. Evidence of the infection may take some time to develop, but antibodies to the viral infection can usually be detected in the blood 2-3 weeks after the tick bite.

Treatment

For a vast majority of patients who become infected, no specific treatment is required. In those that have central nervous system involvement, admission to hospital is required if symptoms are severe. Supportive treatment to reduce symptoms is given. There are no specific anti-viral drugs that can be used against these infections. In individuals in which there is bleeding, blood transfusion or transfusion of other blood products may be required.

Prognosis

Although in a small number of patients infection may be fatal, in the majority of those infected there is a favourable outcome. In those individuals who have central nervous system involvement, complete recovery may take many months or, more rarely, years. It is thus critical that patients be aware of the possibilities of infection and take adequate precautions to reduce tick bites.

What are other worldwide bacterial infections?

As can be seen from Table 4.2, the bacterial infections which can be transmitted by tick bites occur throughout the world. An infection may occur in countries with different climatic conditions, or may be restricted to particular areas of the world. As with viral infections, the list in Table 4.2 emphasises infections which may be imported into Britain. A complete list of worldwide tick-borne bacterial infections would last many pages. Again, it is important to emphasise that individuals returning from a particular country, especially if their lifestyle allowed many tick bites, should seek medical advice about what are the most important tick-borne infections from that country, rather than depend on the completeness of Table 4.2.

Occurrence

As throughout this chapter, infection depends on the season and the likelihood of tick bites. Infections with a worldwide presentation will have different peaks of activity in different countries dependent on the local weather conditions. The widespread distribution of the infections stated in Table 4.2 show the great success of these bacterial agents in managing to survive in parts of the world with quite different climatic conditions.

Symptoms

After an incubation period of 1-14 days, most patients will develop an asymptomatic infection. When symptoms are present, there are three characteristic clinical presentations:

1. An acute illness with fever with a rash. A rash is usually manifest as redness of the skin. In some cases (for example Rocky Mountain Spotted Fever), there is also bleeding into the skin (haemorrhagic fever).

2. An acute illness with relapsing fever. Periods of fever last 2–9 days and alternate with periods without fever lasting 2-4 days. The number of relapses may vary from 1–10 or more. Each period of fever is characterised by rising temperature and finishes with a shaking chill and profuse sweating. The causative agent of this presentation is mainly *Borrelia recurrentis*.

3. An illness called tularaemia (also known as rabbit fever, deer-fly fever, Francis disease) which is usually manifest as skin ulcers. There may be involvement of the eyes, enlarged lymph nodes, and abdominal complaints (pain, diarrhoea and vomiting). The causative organism is *Francisella tularensis*.

Diagnosis

The characteristic symptoms in a patient, a history of tick bite and a knowledge of infections in the country visited are important clues to the diagnosis. Evidence of infection may take some time to develop, but antibodies to the particular bacterial infection can usually be detected in the blood 2–3 weeks after the tick bite. In some cases, it may be possible to grow the bacteria in special laboratory conditions.

Treatment

For many patients, no specific treatment is required. In those that have a more severe illness, specific antibiotic treatment is available, but should only be administered under medical supervision. In individuals with severe bleeding, hospital admission may be required and the individual may require blood transfusion or transfusion of other blood products to stop bleeding.

Prognosis

The majority of those infected will have a favourable outcome. When bleeding is severe, especially if the liver is involved, fatalities may result. Early antibiotic treatment is associated with a very favourable outcome, and hospital admission is critical for speedy diagnosis and management.

5
A REALISTIC APPROACH TO TICK INFECTIONS

Lyme disease symptoms
(Many people will have no symptoms)

- Flu-like illness: malaise, fever, aches.
- Skin rash ('target-like' appearances).
- Joint pain and swelling.
- Nervous system involvement, especially brain, and loss of sensation with tingling in other nerves in the body.
- Chest pains and irregular heart beats.

It is difficult for the general public to have sufficient information and knowledge to develop a realistic approach to many infections. Matters are also often made worse by the media, politicians and self-interested groups. Thus, whether it is salmonella infection in eggs or bovine spongiform encephalopathy (BSE) in meat, it is difficult to know what to do for the best. Often, medical advice on best practice may be fashionable: butter being 'bad' for you, then 'good' for you. Similarly, one should avoid alcohol and then a little red wine is good for you. Indeed, one can get the impression that the medical profession is as confused as the rest of the population in terms of giving good advice.

The main difficulty for the general public is understanding 'risk'. To most individuals, risk is something that can really cause harm. However, the medical use of the word is: 'the risk associated with some potentially harmful factor is defined as the proportion who become ill out of all those exposed to it.' Therefore, it does not mean definitely that the harmful factor always causes disease. Thus, a tick bite is a harmful factor but does not necessarily cause disease.

A further complication is the use of the word 'exposed'. To the general public, if you have been exposed to something, there are inevitable circumstances. Thus, if you are exposed to rain, you get wet. Unfortunately, with infections, it is not as straightforward. If you are exposed to an infection, you do not necessarily become infected. Further, if you do become infected, you may not develop a disease (a state of ill-health) as many who become infected are asymptomatic (have normal health with no complaints). The object of this chapter is to provide information in such a way that the reader can apply the knowledge to his/her particular situation.

How do you become infected?

Large numbers of people will visit areas where there are ticks and where many ticks are infected. Many people live in areas with a high population of ticks. Nevertheless, only a very small number of individuals will become infected. It is really quite difficult to become infected. This fact should reassure most individuals and allow them to enjoy a particular place without undue worry over infections. Further, an informed individual can take appropriate precautions to avoid tick bites and so further reduce the risks of infection.

As explained in Chapter 3, infection depends on the interaction of several factors: the tick, the habitat and the human being. Firstly, as the tick needs to be infected with a particular organism and the majority of ticks are not infected, most ticks cannot transmit infection. The habitat must be conducive to tick survival or else those ticks that are infected will die out. Lastly, the human being needs to be susceptible to that infection. If any of these conditions are not satisfied, there will be no risks of infection to the human being.

Even in cases where these conditions are satisfied, infection will only occur if the human has received a sufficiently large infectious dose (Chapter 3). If there is an insufficient infectious dose, there will be no infection. Simply visiting an area with infected ticks is insufficient for one to worry about receiving an infection. Indeed, even if one has had several tick bites, it is not inevitable that one will become infected. Similarly, even if one has lived in an area where tick bites are a part of life, the majority of the population in that area will not become infected.

As described in Chapter 4, even when there is infection, the results depend on several factors, especially the human's immune system. Of those infected, the vast majority will have an asymptomatic infection; thus, the results of most infections will not be discernible to the individual. Others who are infected will have non-specific symptoms, such as fever, malaise or a flu-like illness. In only a very few individuals will there be a characteristic illness such as distinctive rashes. For all tick-borne infections, the human being is not the primary target. It is important for those visiting and those living in areas with ticks to recognise this fact and not have undue concerns.

Are risks equal?

Many people believe that the risks of getting any infection are equal. This is incorrect. All infectious agents differ in infectiveness, so some organisms are very infectious whereas others are not. This is also compatible with most people's experiences of infections: some infections quickly infect everyone within a family, whereas others may only infect one or two individuals. This difference in those affected is termed an organism's infectiveness, and determines your likelihood of developing a particular infection.

For ticks to transmit an infection to humans, they must first have been infected from other animals. Less commonly, a tick may become infected from a human and transmit an infection to another human. Thus, if large numbers of animals are infected, it seems more likely that human beings will become infected. However, certain infections are very common in animals, but do not necessarily infect ticks to the same extent. Similarly, some infections are very common in animals and ticks, but are uncommon in humans. The explanation is that infectious agents may not easily cross the species' barrier (animals to ticks or ticks to humans). The results of considering the infectiveness of an organism and its ability to cross the species' barrier means that the risks of developing different infections are not equal. Therefore, in Table 4.1 (Chapter 4), the protozoan *babesiosis sp* can produce high infection rates in animals and ticks, but not in humans. Conversely, the bacterium *Borrelia burgdorferi* probably infects animals, ticks and humans to a similar extent. For an individual visiting a tick-infected area for these two diseases, there is a greater chance of developing *Borrelia burgdorferi* infection, and a much smaller chance of developing babesiosis.

Are all infections the same?

For many people, if they develop an infection it is bad news. It is commonly perceived that all infections are the same. As was seen in Chapter 4 (Table 4.1), all infections are quite different in terms of their infectiveness. An infection's importance is usually related to its clinical presentation and the severity of infection. Therefore, Lyme disease is a common infection but is not usually severe in its early disease presentation. In comparison, louping ill is a very uncommon infection, but is very severe in its presentation of an acute illness with encephalitis. For infections such as ehrlichiosis and Lyme disease, there are a large number of individuals who have an asymptomatic infection or an infection with a non-specific illness. This is not seen with infections such as louping ill, Q fever and babesiosis. These latter illnesses do not frequently present with an asymptomatic infection or non-specific clinical findings.

If an individual is visiting a particular area of a country, it is useful to know which infection is likely to be in that place. For individuals who reside in tick-infested areas, there is often local knowledge of places with high tick populations and even whether there are particularly high risks of infection.

This knowledge can be usefully combined with how common the infection is and the usual clinical features of the infection (Chapter 4). Unfortunately, it can be an interesting philosophical question to know if it is better to have an infection which is very common but whose clinical presentation may not be very severe, rather than an infection which is uncommon with a more severe clinical presentation.

If one considers the infectiveness, frequency and clinical presentation of an infectious agent, it is possible to draw several conclusions. Firstly, most infectious organisms do not usually produce very severe clinical presentations in the majority of individuals. Secondly, the infectious agents that have a very severe clinical presentation are usually not as infectious or as common.

However, a difficulty with general statements is that it is quite useful in determining your overall outlook, but is not useful in a particular case. Therefore, if you know that an infection occurs in 1 in 100 patients and another infection occurs in 1 in 100,000 patients, you can say that you are less worried about the latter infection. This would be quite an objective assessment, but it would not be appropriate if you happened to be the one individual involved! If you are the one individual with a very uncommon, severe infection it does not really matter if this state is common or rare. Therefore, infections are not the same, and differ dramatically in their frequency and clinical presentations. These factors influence not only the importance of these infections, but what can be the general public's reasonable approach to them. Simply, one should be particularly worried about certain infections but much less so about others.

Are infection risks greater abroad?

Frequent travel abroad is now a common feature of life for very many individuals. Many perceive that travel abroad is associated with greater infection risks. This perception is partly true: there are more infections in tropical countries compared to temperate countries; and there are more infections in developing countries compared to developed countries. Since many holidays are in tropical and developing countries, there is a greater risk of infection to the traveller. In addition, many individuals travelling to foreign countries would not have been exposed to very many of the indigenous infections; and if one has not been previously infected by an organism, the risk of becoming infected and ill is greater. Therefore, for those travelling abroad, it is a time when there is a greater exposure to infections and the likelihood of becoming infected is higher than remaining in Britain.

For tick-borne infections, the risks of travel abroad are only greater if there is a higher exposure to ticks. This exposure depends on the type of holiday. Obviously, individuals who are trekking in forests have considerably greater risks compared to individuals who are lying on the beach. Activity holidays are therefore a greater risk than the beach/bar/nightclub holiday. Similarly, in this country, individuals who are in towns and cities are at much smaller risk than those who are camping or in rural surroundings. For most individuals going to beach-type holidays, the risks of tick-borne infection are very low.

Important considerations are also the time of year that the holiday is planned; for example the time of peak tick activity has greater risk. The accommodation is also a significant factor. Most package holidays in good hotels represent very little risk. On the other hand, individuals who are backpacking, camping or sleeping rough are at considerably greater risk. In planning a holiday, it is quite important to know what infections might be at their peak in the particular country to be visited. As can be seen in Table 4.2 (Chapter 4), there are very many serious infections which may be acquired whilst travelling abroad. Usually this information is available from the travel agent, and the modern traveller is much better informed than those who went abroad several decades ago.

A recent report has shown that up to 30% of travellers will become ill whilst on holiday. The vast majority of these illnesses are related to the gastro-intestinal tract. In many cases, it is also difficult to separate true infections from over-indulgence in alcohol. In comparison to these risks, the risk of tick-borne infections is very remote. Whilst it is acceptable for an individual on a beach/bar holiday to have little knowledge of tick-borne infections, the same cannot be said for an individual trekking in forests, sleeping rough or camping (Figure 5.1). For those in the latter group, there should be a clear understanding that infection risks are substantial and that appropriate precautions should be taken to avoid tick bites.

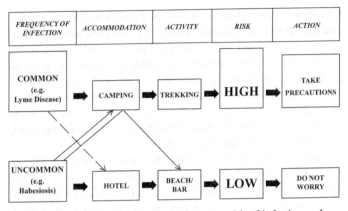

Figure 5.1: Influence of several factors on risk of infection and appropriate action.

What is a realistic approach to tick infection?

A common problem for many individuals is that knowledge of illnesses can create more anxiety than good. In this book, it is hoped that a realistic approach to tick-borne infections can be developed. However, this depends on an individual being able to apply knowledge to his/her situation. Application of knowledge can be very difficult, but is critical in demonstrating a true understanding of the subject. In Figure 5.1, two infections in Britain (Lyme disease, babesiosis) are taken as examples of how other factors may influence the risk of developing an infection. When one knows if the risk of developing an infection is high or low, then the most appropriate course of action can be taken.

For individuals who live in areas of high tick populations, a realistic approach to infection is more difficult. Often, by the nature of their employment, such as dealing with animals or having domestic pets, it is difficult to avoid tick bites.

Fortunately the evidence is that in those who have such repeated exposure to tick bites infection is not common, probably as a result of acquired immunity. Infection risks can also be reduced by sticking to established pathways, especially at times of the year of peak tick activity. There may also be local knowledge that a particular area is associated with some infections. For those living in rural areas, there has always been the need to develop an understanding of nature, of which tick bites and infection are a small part.

As stated in Figure 5.1, those individuals that are at higher risk should take appropriate precautions. The precautions that one can take to avoid tick bites are described in Chapter 6. Many individuals are very reassured by knowledge and can be meticulous about taking precautions. Unfortunately, it should always be remembered that precautions only reduce the risks of infection and do not prevent infection. The concept of no infection only exists for an individual who is living in a plastic bubble. For any individual who is exposed to normal living conditions, there is always a small risk of infection.

It is therefore possible for somebody with high risks of infection who takes all appropriate precautions to reduce his/her risks of infection to something approaching the levels of those who have a low risk of developing infections. However, in Figure 5.1, the appropriate action advised for individuals with low risks of infection is: 'do not worry'. It therefore seems that the same advice can be given to individuals with low risk of infection to those individuals who have a high risk of infection but take appropriate precautions. Is this sensible? The answer is yes.

Another major consideration is that individuals who worry about illnesses or about the possibilities of infection can affect the outcome of infection. Undue concern or worry can by itself depress the functioning of the immune system and therefore the possibility of infection. Therefore, an individual who has a depressed immune system as a result of undue anxiety, concern, or worry will be susceptible to a smaller infectious dose of an organism compared to an individual who is less worried. The message is clear: if the circumstances dictate that one is at high risk, one should take appropriate precautions but should not be particularly worried. Similarly, if one is at low risk one should not worry. It would be very sad if the appropriate actions were taken by an individual, but because of undue anxiety and worry, the fear of developing an infection was realised.

Before the consequences of infections can be properly assessed, it is important to understand that the risks of infection need to be balanced against the pleasure of the activity. Trekking in forests or camping in woodlands are pleasurable activities, and individuals who undertake these activities do so because they are associated with great happiness. For this happiness, they are prepared to suffer discomforts (such as a lack of washing or toilet facilities). The experience of being close to nature and away from all the trappings of civilised life can produce great happiness. Therefore, to develop a realistic approach to tick-borne infections, the great happiness and satisfaction that results from a particular activity and lifestyle must be balanced by the possibility of illness. It is similar to the great happiness that is experienced from having a late night take-away, although it is well recognised that such indulgence may result in an attack of gastro-intestinal disturbance!

6
THE CONTROL OF TICKS ON HUMANS

Tick control

- Worldwide, after a century of pesticide applications, few ticks have been successfully eradicated.

- What drives tick control is the needs of farming. Human health comes second.

- The most effective way to control human infections from ticks is through health education.

- The use of tick repellents is helpful but is no substitute for the daily tick inspection.

- The use of pesticides, the eradication of wildlife hosts or alteration of tick habitats may be useful in localized situations.

The size of the problem

Few parasites have proved as difficult to eradicate as ticks. Control, let alone eradication, of ticks is a formidable task. Unlike most blood-sucking insect pests, ticks are immensely reproductive, remarkably long-lived and can survive starvation for long periods. Attempts to blitz ticks by aerial spraying of pesticides comes up against a further problem—ticks are widely dispersed in forests, pastures and moors and may spend much of the year sheltering, resting, moulting or laying eggs at the base of dense vegetation, largely beyond reach of pesticides. In addition, there is no pesticide which specifically targets ticks—the pesticides marketed against ticks are lethal to spiders and usually to insects and other invertebrates.

The fact remains that after a century of throwing pesticide after pesticide at the problem, few ticks have been successfully eradicated for long periods and then only in limited localities. Ticks, like insects, may in time acquire resistance to pesticides. And even where tick numbers are brought under control, relaxation of the control with free movement of livestock and wildlife frequently results in a new infestation from neighbouring untreated areas.

There is another problem—the fight against ticks, worldwide, is driven primarily by the needs of farming. Undoubtedly, human health has benefited, but this has been largely a by-product of the prior claims of animal health. There are exceptions; in areas such as southern Germany, Switzerland and the eastern USA public concern over Lyme disease in the human population has encouraged the public health authorities to look for inspiration from the agro-chemical and animal health industry.

The solutions

Of all the available approaches to controlling human infections from ticks, the ones which have been of particular benefit are these:

- Health education
- Tick repellents
- Pesticides
- Habitat modification
- Host eradication

Each approach has its merits and drawbacks.

Health education

Public awareness of ticks and tick-borne diseases has developed considerably in recent years largely as a result of Lyme disease, particularly through the Internet. In addition, in Britain, there are feature articles and commentaries on ticks in the magazines for walkers, climbers, campers and naturalists and in the leisure and recreation columns of newspapers. The web-pages, newspaper and magazine articles warn readers of the dangers of tick-borne diseases, and advise on appropriate courses of action.

Advice on ticks and human health also appears from time to time in the farming, forestry and shooting press. The rural industries of farming, shepherding, crofting, game-keeping and stalking are occasionally targeted by one of the Government health or rural affairs departments through bulletins and other publications of limited circulation. And for several years, warnings and advice on ticks have been issued to field workers employed by the Government's environmental agencies such as English Nature or Scottish Natural Heritage, and to university-based field scientists contracted to the Natural Environment Research Council. However, for the majority of people, particularly those seeking an innocent day out in the country, ticks are an unexpected, unseen and often unheeded hazard.

Over recent decades, a very real expectation has developed among holiday-makers, especially those from urban areas, that countryside excursions should be safe and not a health hazard, either to themselves or to their children. In Britain, this group, several million strong, attracted to the countryside to seek their well-earned recreation, will miss out on advice on ticks. At best, some will have read the occasional articles in the broadsheet press on ticks and Lyme disease, but they may be the lucky ones. The North American approach, however, has been very different. The walker or camper, in say Connecticut or Massachusetts, has access to free fact sheets on Lyme disease issued by the state health services linked to websites specifically written for the North American market. Game hunters in Canada and through much of the eastern USA are targeted by tick-repellent manufacturers with information on ticks and tick recognition. For those with specific concerns, detailed information is published by health charities such as the Lyme Disease Foundation. Or the armchair tourist can access the Lyme Disease National Hotline by phone, fax or through the Internet.

In Europe, however, endeavours to improve public awareness of ticks and tick-borne diseases are, by comparison, relatively undeveloped, though improving. If exploring the Internet for advice on ticks and tick-borne diseases, bear in mind that the cultural background, health expectation and medical care and tick biology in the United States, the source of most web entries, is very different from Britain. The reality is that a significant number of North American websites on ticks, and particularly on Lyme disease, are taken up with detail, medical, zoological and ecological, inappropriate to the European situation. A number of sites are scaremongering, inaccurate and written irresponsibly. Other sites give access to a bewildering amount of medical and veterinary clinical information, again often inappropriate to the situation in western Europe with its quite different ticks, different hosts, and different forms of human diseases, including Lyme disease. There are, however, by comparison, a small number of websites written specifically for a European readership. One, as an example, not necessarily a recommendation, is EUCALB (the EU Concerted Action on Lyme Borreliosis) which offers information on European Lyme disease with links to other European sites.

Repellents

Undoubtedly the best way to acquire ticks is to stroll through sheep or deer-grazed grassland at the right season stark naked or at least with legs bared. For those with a taste for it, the kilt is ideal, with or without one's cromag! Combine this with a little sweat and heavy breathing, and ticks will come scuttling. It follows then that the best anti-tick repellent is the solid barrier of clothing—sealed boots, trouser legs tucked into boots or socks drawn over trousers and the wearing of long-sleeved shirts. Light-coloured clothing which shows up ticks is even better. Really determined pin-head sized nymphs, however, will do all they can to find a chink in the clothing barrier, so a thorough daily inspection of one's person may still be needed. However, the combination of a good clothing cover and a daily skin inspection should mean there is no need to resort to repellents.

However, the chemical option is there. The idea is that the chemical repellent applied directly to the skin or to clothing should discourage, preferably entirely ward off, the insect or tick from settling on the skin. The most widely available anti-tick repellent is DEET (diethyl toluamide) usually marketed as an insect repellent against midges and mosquitoes. When applied to clothing, typically socks and trouser legs, it is fairly effective against ticks, and at least one field trial achieved an 80% reduction in tick bites.

In terms of safety, DEET has been around for fifty years and there is no substantial body of evidence that it is harmful to adults when applied directly to the skin, occasionally, and in small quantities. However, DEET, like most repellents, is absorbed by the skin, and passes through the liver before being excreted some hours later. Its use on children is not recommended. Where there is an option it would seem sensible to apply DEET to clothing rather than to the skin—but not, absolutely not, to nylon-based clothing, which many repellents, including DEET, will dissolve.

Permethrin is also marketed as a tick-repellent, though strictly, rather than repel, it actually kills the tick (and many other invertebrates) on contact. This is a powerful synthetic version of the pyrethroids, natural insecticides found in relatives of the chrysanthemum family. A Permethrin-based clothing spray is available from the USA where, it should be carefully noted, its use directly on the skin is *not* authorized. However, both DEET and Permethrin-impregnated clothing quickly lose their anti-tick properties and the treatment may need to be repeated daily for maximum effect. A number of other tick repellents are sold which double up as insect repellents. None have been outstandingly successful.

Each year attractively packaged balms, potions and elixirs are sold, usually pleasantly scented and claiming to ward off ticks and insects. This is a potentially lucrative market, but most of these medicaments do not seem to survive the hard test of consumer approval. There is a fortune to be made if an effective, risk-free tick-repellent were to be marketed. But it has not happened yet.

Pesticides

The question is often asked, why not eradicate ticks through pesticides? Pesticides are widely used to protect humans from the ravages of insect-borne diseases, particularly in the tropics. The military operational problems posed by malaria in World War II led directly to the widespread use of DDT, specifically to combat malaria-carrying mosquitoes. During the late 1940s through to the mid-1960s, DDT and other chlorinated hydrocarbons were widely employed in the war against mosquitoes, tse-tse flies, black flies, lice and other insects implicated in human diseases. The pesticide campaigns often involved aerial spraying over considerable areas, and undoubtedly brought relief to millions of people. The same campaigns, however, proved a disaster to wildlife.

It is a hard fact of life that within a few years of its wide-spread application, insects sooner or later develop resistance to a pesticide. This happened with DDT by the early 1950s, within seven years of being introduced. Ticks too have developed resistance to a number of pesticides. Today we have ticks which are resistant to pyrethroids and organophosphates.

Anti-tick pesticides are widely used to control ticks on livestock (see chapter 7) and may bring incidental benefits to human health. The reason that pesticides are not targeted against ticks solely for the benefit of human health is that humans are not the main target of the tick, but form, at very best, an occasional opportunity to secure a blood meal. This may be no succour to the hill walker or forester who subsequently contracts Lyme disease, however. Anti-tick pesticides have sometimes been used as part of a (human) public health campaign in localized hot-spots for Lyme disease, especially in recreational areas, near built-up areas and on military bases, mainly in the eastern USA. However, the considerable environmental risk and public resistance to broad-scale spraying makes this approach limited in its application.

Habitat modification

Perhaps the most widespread method of controlling ticks is to modify the natural environment. Targeted habitats include the areas around recreation parks and campsites. Habitat modification usually involves altering the form and composition of vegetation by mowing, burning, application of herbicides and by clearance of scrub and trees. The principle is simple enough—to create a habitat which does not offer ticks a sanctuary to lay eggs, to rest, to over-winter, to allow questing or to secure a blood meal. The ultimate tick-unfriendly habitat would be a large area covered in concrete and free of live-stock, small mammals and all plant life—a city centre car park, for example. Second best would be a regularly mown short grass lawn.

On a local scale, undoubtedly, habitat modification does work. This approach has been widely applied in residential areas on the edges of towns and villages, particularly in New England where there is public concern over the presence of Lyme disease-carrying ticks. Often the approach used is to alter the habitat so as to discourage deer and other mammals. Typically, on the outskirts of residential areas or of camp sites, encroaching woodland is cut down with regular mowing of vegetation alongside footpaths. The trouble is that vegeta-tion does not stand still and the habitat management regime needs to be applied frequently each and every year. Small mammals, notoriously, will often rapidly re-colonize areas, particularly after burning and mowing, bringing in their own fresh complement of ticks.

Host eradication

Another approach is not to tackle the tick itself but to deal with the tick's food source—the principle being that if the tick is deprived of a blood meal for long enough it will die of starvation. This has been the principle underpinning many host eradication campaigns for decades.

Repeated observations have confirmed that where there is a high density of hosts—deer, sheep, cattle, field mice and so on, there tend to be large populations of ticks. The introduc-tion of extensive flocks of sheep into the Scottish Highlands in the nineteenth century brought with it anecdotal evidence of a large increase in tick-infested pastures followed by the tick-borne disease louping-ill. More recently, in the USA, attempts have been made to reduce the incidence of Lyme disease by reducing deer herd sizes. Trials in Cape Cod, bounded on three sides by the Atlantic, however, only achieved a significant reduction in Lyme disease when almost all of the deer had been eliminated. Indeed, there was some evidence that as the number of deer declined, so hungry ticks began plaguing humans. In another Massachusetts experiment, this time on an off-shore island, all of the resident tick-infested white-tailed deer were shot in an attempt to eradicate Lyme disease. Unhappily, the adult ticks, deprived of their deer, simply moved to racoons.

In recreational areas in parts of Germany, Austria and Switzerland, deer exclusion fences have been erected specifically in an attempt to reduce the incidence of Lyme disease. The approach has limited application and may be counterproductive, particularly when the original attraction of the area for visitors was the very sight of deer!

Anti-tick measures against livestock may be far more effective than attempts to control ticks on wildlife, though not always. Relaxation of veterinary controls has seen the spread of tick-borne diseases into Europe. The origin of tick-borne human encephalitis in western Europe is believed to have been the movement of cattle from eastern Europe. Mediterranean spotted fever appears to have spread northwards on the backs of tick-infested dogs. The vets cannot be blamed, however, for the spread of human haemorrhagic fever from Ukraine. This fever is thought to have spread to western Europe through infected ticks on hares and migratory birds.

The way forward

For most people not working in the countryside, ticks and tick-borne diseases are a relatively new phenomenon. After all, the increasingly familiar name 'Lyme disease' was only coined a little more than thirty years ago. In Britain, publicity in newspapers and particularly the farming and hillwalking press has done much to improve awareness of ticks. In time the public health authorities may add their weight to education campaigns. But for the immediate future, it is almost certain that we humans will have to remain content with the hard reality that the control of ticks in Britain, as in much of Europe and the rest of the world, is in the hands of those concerned primarily with animal health. Short of a major epidemic, it is unlikely that limited public health resources will be diverted to protecting humans from ticks.

Sole reliance on repellents or pesticides, or on large scale habitat modification, does not seem to be the way forward. Recent changes, or forecasts of change, in the scale and form of livestock farming could well influence the size of the tick population on pasture land and rough grazing. The expansion of forested areas and the exclusion of red deer from large areas of the Scottish Highlands will be watched with interest. Changes in climate, particularly rainfall and temperature, are likely to affect the questing and biting behaviour of our resident tick populations, particularly the sheep-tick with its distinct patterns of seasonal activity. All of these changes will have an effect on the incidence of ticks biting humans, and inevitably on tick-borne disease. Until we know more about the changes in patterns of tick activity and the incidence of tick-borne diseases in Britain, for the foreseeable future there will be no substitute for education—authoritative practical information on ticks and tick-borne diseases and how to avoid them. What is needed is not just a health warning for the serious hill walker, climber, shooter, fisher, farmer, crofter or forester, but for all who seek healthy and rewarding recreation in the countryside.

And if all else fails—what to do if a tick bites!

How to remove a tick

- Ticks should be removed from the body promptly but, more important, correctly.
- Use tweezers, not finger nails.
- Lay the tweezers firmly on the skin close to the tick's mouth parts.
- Grasp the tick and pull it up and out steadily without twisting.
- Clean the wound.
- Watch the wound over subsequent days.

At the end of the day, regardless of repellents and pesticides, if a tick bites it must be removed! For the reasons given in previous chapters the risk of infection can be greatly reduced if the tick is removed *promptly*. The procedure is simple and effective, provided three key points are borne in mind.

1. The tick has a pair of barbed headpieces which are firmly anchored into the wound during feeding. In addition, the tick secretes a cement-like substance which binds the head firmly to the wound. The result is that ticks are more likely to break up if improperly handled, so leaving the head part and saliva embedded in the skin.

2. Ticks can be readily removed at home or in the field, and it is *not* necessary to call out the doctor or attend Accident and Emergency Hospital Clinics! People who work with animals or pursue rural occupations in tick-infested areas are well used to removing ticks.

3. A most important point, the tick should be removed *completely* and parts of the headpiece should *not* be left in the flesh. Complete removal is usually not difficult. All that is needed is a pair of tweezers—preferably fine-pointed straight tweezers.

The tip of the tweezers should be placed on either side of the tick's mouth parts (the place where the tick is attached to the skin) laying the tweezers *as close to the skin as possible.* Gently but firmly close the tweezers and—steadily—pull the tick straight out. It is quite unnecessary to twist while pulling —indeed twisting the tick is one way of breaking off the barbed headpiece and leaving it in the flesh.

If a pair of tweezers are not immediately available it is better to wait and remove the tick later that day. Attempting to remove a tick with finger nails should be avoided—but if it has to be done then use a paper tissue or clean handkerchief to avoid contact with potentially infected tick fluids. If parts of the head are left in the wound, a thorough attempt should be made to extract the pieces in the same way as a splinter would be removed, using tweezers or, if necessary, a sterilized needle. Having removed the tick, the wound should be cleaned with an antiseptic cream, or alcohol, the tweezers disinfected and the hands washed thoroughly with soap and water.

Do *not* prick out, crush or burn the tick, as this may well cause the tick to release its fluids into the wound, possibly under pressure. And do not attempt to swathe or smother the tick in creams, ointments, soap, petroleum jelly, whisky, nail varnish or other liquids. Ticks are most unlikely to release their hold on the flesh, particularly if they have been attached for some hours.

Young children should *not* be encouraged to pull out ticks but should seek help from an adult. A watch should be kept on the bite over the following days. The area around the bite may redden for a few days but this should soon clear up. If it does not clear up seek medical advice. Finally, there is no substitute for vigilance. A daily inspection for ticks during the tick season should be a routine practice.

There is at least one patented tick-remover on the market, designed originally for small animal veterinary use, a miniature two-pronged hook or claw, in plastic, shaped to slide under and around the tick. Designed for use on pets, limited-scale trials on humans show a potential for wider application.

7

TICKS—THEIR IMPACT ON LIVESTOCK AND WILDLIFE

Effects of tick-borne diseases

- Epidemics of tick-borne diseases in livestock can destroy whole herds and flocks.
- Many livestock diseases can be transmitted to humans.
- Large-scale and ambitious campaigns to eradicate ticks have largely given way to reducing tick numbers to tolerable levels.
- A few livestock diseases can be controlled through vaccinations.
- Traditionally, tick-borne diseases of livestock are contained by the use of organophosphate and pyrethroid dips. These are now being supplemented by new chemicals, such as the avermectins. If used properly these can be very effective, although over-use and misuse can be harmful to a range of organisms in the environment.
- A tick-specific pesticide has yet to be found; all pesticides affect wildlife.
- Tick-borne diseases also affect wildlife and can occasionally lead to high levels of mortality.

The background

Humans can be justly concerned about Lyme disease and other tick-borne diseases, but these pale into insignificance when compared with tick-borne diseases of animals, with not even our domestic pets escaping, as we will see in the following chapter. The tick-borne diseases of animals consist of a very complex set of several diseases whose agents may be bacterial, viral or protozoal (single-celled parasites more complex than bacteria); all of these can be transmitted by ticks. Ticks acquire the disease agents while they feed on infected animals and subsequently transfer them to other animals when they move to another host—these animals will, themselves, then become infected. Furthermore, the animal becomes the disease sink or 'reservoir' for the disease—the primary reservoirs are usually mammalian wildlife or livestock, but birds and reptiles can also play a role.

Being opportunistic creatures, ticks are also not averse to feeding from humans as you have already read, and also from our pets, passing infections on to these groups, which become mini-reservoirs themselves. Often, the same disease agent can infect both animals and humans, but may produce a different range of symptoms in each. In some cases, an infected tick doesn't even need to take a bloodmeal to spread the disease—instead, the bacteria or other parasite may be passed from one generation of tick to another 'trans-stadially'—that is, between the different life stages of the tick, including through its ovaries and into its fertilised eggs.

Worldwide, the number and range of diseases carried by ticks exceeds those of all other invertebrates, bar none.

Livestock: the biggest challenge

A herd of cattle or a flock of sheep is nothing more than a free meal-ticket to a hungry tick. The optimal conditions to support a large population of well-fed ticks (and to achieve maximal disease transmission if either the ticks or the animals are infected) are achieved when susceptible animals are herded together in large numbers. Few better conditions exist for ticks than in modern livestock farming. While tick-borne diseases are present throughout the world, they are most numerous and exert their greatest impact in tropical and sub-tropical regions. In many of these regions, livestock are more than just providers of milk and meat—they are highly productive assets, for example, being used for jobs such as ploughing and for transport. In many African countries cattle are described as 'banks on hooves', and it follows that losing cattle is a loss of both wealth and status.

The most important tick-transmitted diseases associated with livestock have been present in largely resistant wild animal herds for thousands of years, and it was not until new, susceptible stock was introduced alongside these (mainly from Europe) that problems arose. Despite the diseases being recognised for at least a century, ticks are still the major impediments to efficient livestock production in many countries, resulting in a staggering global economic toll in terms of meat and milk production. Approximately 80 percent of the world's cattle population of 1,281 million are at risk from ticks and tick-borne diseases. Estimates at the end of the twentieth century put the world-wide cost of tick-borne diseases for cattle alone at $10,000 million annually! This is a challenge that is still to be properly addressed and requires a full understanding of the biology of both the tick and the diseases it carries, together with an appreciation of the socio-economic environment in which the diseases are exerting an effect.

For every tick which completes its life cycle on an animal, there is an estimated loss of blood of 1–3 millilitres—this makes them very efficient transmitters of diseases, but they can also cause significant economic damage in other ways. For example, the irritation resulting from tick infestations can damage hides and also, through the wounds that tick bites cause, the animals are often more susceptible to secondary bacterial infections and even screw-worms—parasitic flies which lay their eggs in open wounds, where the hatching larvae can cause considerable damage and distress to the animal.

There are actually over 60 different tick-borne disease agents which can infect livestock throughout the world, although far fewer are recognised as being of economic significance. The 'big four', which affect a range of both domesticated and wild animals across the world and dominate the veterinary text-books, are babesiosis, theileriosis, anaplasmosis and cowdriosis. The following short accounts outline the severity and economic importance of each of these.

The 'big four'

Babesiosis

Babesiosis, or tick fever, is a disease of domestic and wild animals that occurs in a number of different forms, resulting in a variety of regional names. It is characterised by a fever and extensive breakdown of red blood cells—this is often seen as a reddish tinge to the urine, explaining one of its names; 'redwater fever'. Severe anaemia frequently follows, which can be fatal. The disease is caused by protozoan *Babesia* parasites, which are transmitted by a variety of tick species. There are at least 14 distinct species of *Babesia*, with the most economically damaging being *Babesia argentina* and *Babesia bigemina*. These are both widespread in tropical and sub-tropical countries wherever *Boophilus* cattle ticks occur, which are their main vector.

One peculiar gap in the distribution of *Babesia argentina* has led to a novel method of protection from babesiosis—the introduction of resistant cattle. Despite *Boophilus* ticks occurring in East Africa, there are few reports of babesiosis in this region. This turns out to be because zebu cattle, which are widespread here, are significantly less susceptible to the clinical effects of *Babesia* infection (although not to the infection itself) than cattle of European breeds. The humped zebu first arrived in Africa from Asia around 1500 BC. Today, together with their crosses (for example, sanga cattle; crosses between zebu and European species) they are being increasingly exploited as a means of control of babesiosis. The introduction of resistant zebu cattle to Australia has revolutionised the control of cattle ticks on that continent and a similar approach is becoming increasingly important in Africa and the Americas.

Infections caused by *Babesia bigemina* have been written into North American history alongside the romantic image of the American cowboy and the Texan cattle drives. Cattle have been reared in Texas since the eighteenth century, when the Spanish attempted to establish missions and domesticate the Indians. These early cattle were mainly Spanish, with horns up to 2.5 metres wide. However, as the cattle drives headed northwards it soon became obvious that they were associated with a lethal disease—in June 1868 it was reported that a 'very subtle and terribly fatal disease' had broken out among cattle in Illinois. The disease, associated in cattle with listlessness, twitching and gnashing of teeth, was reported to be 'fatal in every instance', resulting in financial ruin for the cattle ranchers. 15,000 head of cattle were lost which, in today's terms, would equate to a loss in excess of a billion dollars. Before the disease was properly diagnosed as Texas cattle fever (also called 'Spanish fever'), some weird and wonderful theories were proposed—including that the Spanish longhorns ate poisonous plants that for some reason did not harm them but did make their wastes extremely toxic, and that accidental ingestion of these by non-immune cows led to the sickness. Following tick eradication programmes, babesiosis is now considered an exotic cattle disease in the United States, although its threat still stalks the plains, particularly from imported infected animals.

Theileriosis

Like babesiosis, theileriosis is a protozoan disease which has its place in history due to its disastrous consequences. Globally, a number of different *Theileria* pathogens which cause the disease exist in different hosts, but by far the most pathogenic and economically important is *Theileria parva*—the cause of East Coast fever in cattle (also known as 'corridor disease' and 'January disease') that swept through Africa at the end of the nineteenth century. Today its distribution is limited to eastern and southern Africa, and in many areas it is the most important cattle killer. The tick vector is *Rhipicephalus appendiculatus*, which normally attaches to the ear and so is often called the 'brown ear tick'. The African buffalo is a significant reservoir source for theileriosis, remaining infective to ticks for at least three years, and it is in these animals where disease epidemics in domesticated cattle probably started.

The earliest written records of East Coast fever come from the 1569 diaries of a Jesuit missionary, Father Monclaro, but it was with European settlers spreading into Africa in search of gold and diamonds during the nineteenth century that the disease came to the forefront. These pioneers also brought their highly susceptible cattle, releasing them onto the grasslands alongside the buffalo. East Coast fever rapidly spread through the newcomers and continued southwards over the next few years, leading to devastating losses. The greatest losses occurred in 1901, coinciding with the Anglo–Boer war of 1899–1902, when cattle were imported to support the war effort.

Despite vigorous control programmes (mainly through cattle dipping), East Coast fever remains a major constraint to cattle development—the annual cost of the disease in Africa is estimated at $200 million.

Anaplasmosis

Anaplasmosis is caused by a group of bacteria that invade and multiply in the red blood cells of a variety of hosts, including cattle, sheep, goats and other wild ruminants. The most important species again infects cattle; *Anaplasma marginale* causes bovine anaplasmosis, which is characterised in the acute form by fever, anaemia, general weakness and depression. Mortality levels can be as high as 70% during severe outbreaks but even without death, the economic impacts of abortions, weight loss, decreased milk production and infertility in bulls can be huge. Young calves appear to have an innate resistance to the disease, with cattle over 3 years old succumbing to the most severe form. Animals surviving an acute attack will make a slow recovery but they also become reservoirs for life—and so act as a source of infection for susceptible animals. The bacterium may be biologically transmitted by 20 or more species of ticks (i.e. the disease undergoes its development within the tick) but it may also be mechanically transmitted by a variety of biting fly species, particularly horse flies—the disease particles being picked up on the fly's mouthparts as it feeds, which can then contaminate other animals as the fly moves off to feed from a different host.

Anaplasmosis has a very wide distribution in tropical, subtropical and even temperate zones. In fact today it can be found nearly worldwide, and epidemics can wipe out large numbers of cattle at one go—for example, in 1986 an epidemic in North America resulted in a loss of 100,000 cattle before the disease was brought under control.

Cowdriosis

Cowdriosis, or heartwater, is an important African disease of cattle, sheep and goats. It is transmitted trans-stadially (from adults through their eggs to the next generation) by several species of *Amblyomma* tick, of which *Amblyomma variegatum* (or the 'tropical bont tick') is the most widespread. The first record of the disease was probably made in South Africa by the Afrikaans pioneer, Louis Trichard. In an entry in his diary on 9 March 1838 he mentions a fatal disease, 'nintas', amongst his sheep, approximately 3 weeks after a massive tick infestation. Indigenous to the African continent, the disease now appears to have spread into some of the Caribbean islands, where *Amblyomma variegatum* has been introduced, apparently with a shipment of cattle from Senegal into the French Antilles in the 1830s. Since that time, heartwater has spread throughout the islands and causes significant concerns regarding its possible introduction into the American mainland with livestock carrying infected ticks. Similar concern is also associated with the importation from Africa of tick-infested reptiles, since several species of *Amblyomma* tick that feed on reptiles (including tortoises) can carry the heartwater pathogens.

The disease is caused by a bacterium, *Cowdria ruminantium* which accumulates in the blood vessels; particularly in the capillaries of the brain. Infected animals often show a characteristic twitching of the muscles, a lack of co-ordination and, very quickly, death follows. Fluid leakage through blood capillaries accumulates in the body, including around the heart—giving the origin of the 'heartwater' name.

There is a lack of information on the true impact of cowdriosis, but certainly in areas of Africa, it is a very important obstacle in the development and upgrading of livestock farming.

Prevention of these potentially lethal diseases still relies primarily on chemical control—mainly pesticide dips and sprays. In some cases treatment can be achieved through antibiotics, but often the use of these is impractical. Much of the farming under threat is carried out under range conditions, over often thousands of hectares, and the effective treatment of animals under these circumstances is largely impossible.

B-list tick-borne diseases

Outside of the top four conditions described above, ticks transmit many, many more diseases to livestock, which can be just as important in their own right. As above, the distribution of many of these is spreading along with their tick hosts and their vertebrate bloodmeals. These include a series of tick-borne viral diseases, many of which are named according to where they were first recognised. An example is Nairobi sheep disease, now known to be identical with Ganjam virus in India. This is a widespread tick-borne disease in east Africa and associated with livestock-trading in Kenya's major cities. While resident sheep and goats are generally immune, severe outbreaks can occur in susceptible animals moved to these areas, which commonly have a poor prognosis. Another example is African swine fever virus, which is a highly contagious disease of pigs and for which ticks of the genus *Ornithodoros* are thought to be important in its transmission. The virus resists inactivation, persisting in meat up to 15 weeks, processed hams for up to 6 months and for up to one month in contaminated pig pens. First identified in Kenya in the 1920s, African swine fever is now endemic in most of Southern Africa and has spread into Europe, where wild boar populations are proving to be an excellent reservoir, with resulting outbreaks in pigs in France, Italy, Malta, Belgium and Holland.

In these European areas, as well as disease transmission from *Ornithodoros* ticks, direct transmission through contact with sheds contaminated with infective secretions is also very important. Spread of the disease by the ingestion of products from infected pigs is also an important way that the virus spreads to new countries—for example, through pigs being fed illegally imported pig meats and other pig products. The current theory regarding the introduction of the disease into Europe is that sewage from an aircraft coming from Angola in 1957 introduced the disease into Portugal, from where it spread through Western Europe.

The UK and closer to home

Tick populations in the UK and northern Europe can be huge, particularly where sheep and cattle are grazing. In one recent study, exceptionally high values were consistently recorded from the vegetation associated with paths used by sheep (and also by human walkers), with estimates exceeding 400,000 ticks per hectare. It is not unusual to see very high numbers of ticks on sheep in heavily grazed and vegetated areas, such as the Scottish Highlands. In many of these areas sheep farming is central to the livelihood of many small farmers and crofters, and hence it is important for them to be aware of the potential threats posed by ticks to their animals.

Tick-borne fever

Tick-borne fever (or ehrlichiosis) is widespread amongst domestic sheep and cattle in north-west Europe, with relatively mild effects in the majority of animals. In sheep, the main clinical sign is a sudden fever, lasting for 4-10 days. Other signs are usually either absent or mild, although the animals generally appear dull and may lose weight. In addition, respiratory and pulse rates are usually increased, and a cough often develops. In cattle, the disease is known as pasture fever in many parts of Europe, including Finland, Norway, Austria, Spain and Switzerland. Again, as with sheep, the symptoms of the disease are usually mild, resulting in an annual minor epidemic when dairy cows are turned out to pasture in the spring and early summer. Within days, the cows are dull and depressed, with a significant loss of appetite and reduction in milk yield. As with sheep, affected cows usually also suffer from breathing difficulties and coughing.

In both sheep and cattle, tick-borne fever can result in miscarriage in pregnant ewes and cows. Also, in rams and bulls which have been bought from tick-free areas and then put into tick-infested pastures, tick-borne fever may cause them to become temporarily sterile and, therefore, useless for the job that they were bought for!

Probably the most significant effect of tick-borne fever infection is an impairment of the immune system. Particularly in young animals, this can result in reduced growth, but most importantly, it increases susceptibility to more serious diseases such as the tick-borne encephalitis, louping ill.

Louping ill

For many years, louping ill was considered to be a disease which affected cattle and sheep in northern England and Scotland. However, it has now been reported from Bulgaria, Turkey, Spain, Norway, Russia and the Czech Republic. This viral disease (which is also known as 'trembling-ill') is of greatest veterinary importance as a disease of sheep. It is transmitted by the sheep tick, *Ixodes ricinus*. The outcome of infection in sheep is unpredictable, with some infected flocks showing no clinical disease, whereas in others, severe clinical symptoms occur and death is frequently seen. However, louping ill also affects wild grouse. Most wild birds that are infected will die, and therefore, in some areas, the purpose of control of louping-ill is actually to reduce grouse mortality, and hence enhance the economic return from sporting activities.

Louping ill is characterised by fever and lethargy, in addition to muscular incoordination, tremors and posterior paralysis—all of which contribute to a leaping (or 'louping') gait. These signs, however, don't appear until 6-10 days after infection. Coma and death can follow. Commonly, between 5% and 60% of infected sheep develop clinical signs—why this is so variable is not clear, although it is thought that stresses, such as herding and severe weather, can increase the likelihood of the disease developing.

Those animals which survive louping ill infection will develop high levels of antibodies in their blood which will protect them for the rest of their lives. This protection will also be passed onto lambs in the ewe's colostrum (fed to the lamb in the first few hours of life) for their first 2 months of life. Those lambs that are not protected (such as those rejected at birth and not receiving the essential colostrum), however, are most susceptible, together with yearlings which are kept for breeding. As with all tick-borne diseases, if louping ill is suspected in a herd of sheep, a diagnosis should be sought from a vet. If an infection is confirmed, it is possible to vaccinate (particularly ewes kept for breeding) and although this is expensive, it is extremely effective and will provide good protection for at least two years.

There are reports of farmers, and other people working with sheep, suffering an encephalitis, caused by the same louping ill virus as above. Very, very rarely, infections can be fatal in humans. Hence, care should be taken if handling potentially infected animals and carcasses. In addition, ticks attaching to people should be removed as quickly as possible to reduce the likelihood of any disease transmission.

Tick management: is there a solution?

Tick control is an extremely difficult issue, compounded by a whole range of factors, including cultural, environmental, financial and political ones. It has also become an international issue, as relaxations in trade barriers make the movement of animals between countries and continents increasingly easy. Also, cheaper air travel, combined with an affluent society always looking out for the next bizarre pet, encourages the importation of exotic animals, which may be infested with foreign tick species.

We now know that the eradication of ticks is not feasible or desirable. Firstly, the cost would be enormous, and also, once started, any eradication programme would need to be continued, since livestock are likely to lose their immunity to tick-transmitted diseases if they are not re-exposed. While exposed to a low level of infection, animals will build up antibodies to a disease which provide some level of protection (in the same way that vaccination does). Complete eradication, however, would remove this stimulus and leave animals very susceptible if they did come into contact with an infected tick. The consequences in these situations could be disastrous. This was seen in Zimbabwe during the liberation wars of the 1970s, when the breakdown of dipping caused losses from tick-borne diseases approaching one million head of cattle.

Integrating tick and tick-borne disease control for success

The practice of intensive tick control through insecticide dipping spread rapidly throughout Africa following the introduction of exotic cattle breeds—in fact, in many African countries it was enforced through legislation. In the past two decades, however, it has become apparent that intensive tick control is expensive and not always in the best interest of the animals. The assumption that indigenous livestock require the same level of protection as imported breeds has meant that, for the last 100 years, millions of resistant cattle have been dipped regularly for the sake of a small proportion of susceptible stock. This has lead to the loss both of resistance to ticks, and also much of the inherent immunity to tick-borne diseases.

There have been many studies, both scientific and economic, of tick management, and countries are being actively encouraged to intensify their efforts to control ticks and tick-borne diseases. The main future objectives are improvements in tick control, disease treatment and livestock protection through immunisation. Of greatest importance is the integration of all of these aspects into effective disease control programmes.

Preserving natural immunity

It is important that the natural immunity of cattle herds in particular is re-established, either through the re-introduction of resistant strains or through immunisation wherever possible. A common practice today is to make use of the fact that zebu cattle are more resistant to tick infestation than European breeds, resulting in the widespread introduction of zebu cross-breeds with increased resistance. Experimental observations on cattle have shown that less than 1% of ticks feed successfully on indigenous, resistant cattle breeds, whereas more than 50% feed completely on exotic breeds.

Some diseases are easier to immunise against than others. Currently, effective methods of immunisation are available for only a few diseases, including babesiosis and anaplasmosis, and even these have limitations. Significant progress has also been made with other diseases through the vaccination of herds with extracts made from ticks. Current trials are concentrating in particular on theileriosis, using an 'infection and treatment' method—animals are injected with infective particles derived from ticks and then are treated during the early part of the incubation period with an anti-parasitic drug (often in cattle feed or incorporated into salt blocks). Effectively, the treated livestock produce their own anti-tick immune response before they are bitten by a tick. Ticks which then try to feed from these animals have difficulty drawing blood and eventually die. Infection and treatment is applied on a fairly large scale in some countries such as Zambia, and on a more limited scale in a few other countries. Although it is a rather crude method, the immunity it provides against theileriosis is long-lasting, but on the other hand, immunised animals remain reservoirs and so can act as a source of infection to other animals. There are also numerous technical difficulties with this method, and current research activity is directed towards the development of effective molecular vaccines. Unlike developing a vaccine against a relatively simple virus or bacteria, the minute worm-like protozoan causing theileriosis is far more complex, and sophisticated vaccines that can deal with it are still some years off. For the time being, vaccination is expensive and requires repeated administration, and we must wait for technological advances in molecular vaccines to overcome these issues.

Eradication—the tick or the host?

Some tick-borne diseases have been apparently eradicated by the elimination of the ticks themselves, particularly in the Americas—for example, the eradication of Texas cattle fever (babesiosis) in the United States by removing the *Boophilus* tick vector. In general, widespread tick or tick-borne disease eradication is not encouraged, particularly in developing countries, for fear of the programmes being interrupted, leaving behind large populations of susceptible livestock. The success of tick eradication will also be highly dependent on how isolated an infested area is and whether it is feasible to prevent tick re-infestation—in practice this can often involve quarantine regulations and the costly re-application of control methods. Some countries still favour tick eradication on a regional basis —for example in areas of Australia threatened with babesiosis and anaplasmosis—but only in conjunction with immunisation.

Even with the necessary resources for national eradication efforts, programmes can still fail. One of the reasons for this may be the abundance of wild reservoir hosts for a particular tick species, making tick eradication almost impossible. This was behind a number of drastic attempts at the beginning of the twentieth century to eradicate these hosts in order to break the tick's life cycle, for example the culling in 1911 of a whole range of small animals, including squirrels and chipmunks, to control Rocky Mountain spotted fever in Montana, USA. Fortunately, the authorities eventually saw sense, recognising that the practice was ineffective, inhumane and expensive. Indeed, for any species of tick that has a wide host range, this line of attack is never going to succeed. For example, our own sheep tick will feed from a huge array of rodents, other small mammals and a variety of birds. More humane approaches to such problems are currently being investigated in the United States, where one of the main hosts for ticks transmitting Lyme disease is white-tailed deer. In a programme named 'Target Lyme Disease', a scratching post for these deer is topically treated with insecticide—to date, more than 90% of local deer have been exposed to the device and tick numbers on them have been cut to a tenth of their previous tick burden.

Targeting the tick

Ticks themselves are difficult to control, since they spend so much of their time off the host, and even when on it, have such limited movement that the chances of them coming into contact with insecticides on the animal are minimal. Measures aimed directly at the tick itself come under three main headings: 'chemical', 'biological control' and what for here will be called 'novel approaches'.

Chemical control

The control of ticks through the application of chemical pesticides fairly closely mirrors the development of these organic chemicals. At the outset of chemical applications against ticks, 70 years ago, water-soluble forms of arsenic were used in dipping vats. The cheapness and stability of the products resulted in their widespread use—indeed, it was arsenic dips that successfully eradicated *Boophilus* cattle ticks from the southern United States. Unfortunately, the lethality of the compounds to ticks was also passed on to the treated livestock and the farmers, and so these compounds were phased out in the 1940s in favour of a new group, the chlorinated hydrocarbons. This cheap, widely available group of pesticides included DDT, the accumulation of which in the environment and the resulting disastrous consequences for wildlife are well documented. The compounds also created residues that remained in the tissues of treated livestock for many years. Their use in the United States and Western Europe was finally banned in the early 1970s. On the African continent it was the development by the ticks of strong resistance to the organochlorines which gave the primary push for a transfer to the use of organophosphate pesticides (or 'OPs'), which became available in the 1960s and were less persistent in the

environment than DDT. However, their residual effectiveness was usually shorter than that of chlorinated hydrocarbons,
and the risk of causing acute toxicity in livestock was greater.
Several tick species are also now known to be resistant to
organophosphorous pesticides. Today, where organophosphates
are still used for tick control, this is often carried out in
combination with synthetic pyrethroids, such as permethrin—
a copy of natural pyrethrum, which was first isolated from
chrysanthemums for its insecticidal properties. Synthetic forms
of pyrethrum were available from the 1970s, although the
plant's properties were mentioned much earlier in early Chi-
nese history. The plant was brought to Europe from China
along the silk routes in ancient times, and pyrethrum powders
were used by armies from the time of Napoleon to the Second
World War to protect against lice. The synthetic forms persist well on the coat or skin, and so are of significant value
against skin parasites such as ticks. They also have a low
mammalian toxicity, although are very poisonous to fish and
crustaceans. Unfortunately, resistance to pyrethroids was recognised in ticks within 10 years of their introduction into
control programmes.

The newest chemical hope for tick control is a group of
broad spectrum anti-parasitic drugs called avermectins, introduced onto the international animal health market in 1981,
with the main product being Ivermectin. In Britain it is approved for the use in cattle, sheep, goats, pigs and horses.
The drug is absorbed systemically after administration and is
excreted mainly in the faeces. Being insecticidal, residues of
Ivermectin in cow dung can reduce the number and variety of
insects which make it their home. Hence, although the
avermectins have a short persistence in the environment, they
can have a significant localised impact. This has caused concern, particularly because of the potential knock-on effect on

those species of birds that rely on cow dung as an important insect food-source. Furthermore, their long-term effects, particularly secondary impacts within the ecosystem, remain to be fully determined, and further research is required in this area. At present, these concerns are offset by the fact that Ivermectin is very lethal against ticks, and at sub-lethal doses it slows down ticks' maturing and inhibits both egg laying and blood feeding. In fact, it is rare today to go into a farmers' supplier or veterinary surgeon and not see advertisements for avermectin-based anti-parasitic products.

All of these chemical pesticides, while still routinely used in sheep and cattle dips, are now incorporated in newer and easier methods of application. This is helping farmers to move away from the 'spray-it-all' attitude that has prevailed in the past, often leading to increased livestock susceptibility to tick-borne diseases, together with potential hazards to the health of the operator, as highlighted in the contentious issue of organophosphate sheep dips in the UK. Newer applications include ear tags, neck bands, tail bands and pour-ons. Ivermectin is administered via injection, implants and also in food; a recent trial in Kenya with an Ivermectin formulation which broke down slowly in the stomach, from where it entered the blood stream, provided three months of protection against tick infestation.

Biological control

Biological control is the use of a natural enemy to control a target pest. In the same way that cats chase mice and dogs chase cats, all animals have their own enemies, but the problems lie, firstly, in identifying these and, secondly, deploying them in an effective manner. In the field of arthropod pest control, there are few true examples of successful biological control, and where they do occur, they can rarely cope with pest numbers in epidemic proportions, as are so often seen with ticks. Both ecologists and entomologists have searched unsuccessfully over many years for biological agents for the control of ticks, including supposed natural enemies such as parasitic wasps, wolf spiders and foraging guinea fowl. These have all been found to be either highly localised in their impacts on tick survival, or entirely ineffective. For example, in Africa, infestations of ticks on livestock and wild ungulates may be reduced by oxpeckers—birds that feed on attached ticks—but only as part of an organised disease management programme, including immunisation and pesticide treatments. Perhaps the largest attempts at biological control in the field were carried out in the USA and Russia during the 1920s, when parasitic wasps were released into areas heavily infested with ticks. It was known that the wasps would lay their eggs in the bodies of ticks and that the hatched wasp larvae would effectively eat the ticks from the inside out. This seemed like an excellent approach, until it was realised that the wasp populations would not survive for long enough to make it successful.

However, some glimmer of hope now appears to be showing, particularly with products based on naturally-occurring fungi, isolated from the soil and, when applied to insect pests, causing their death by effectively invading and slowly eating their tissues. In the USA there is a commercially-available fungal preparation for the control of termites, and research is being directed towards extending this to ticks for the control of Lyme disease. Laboratory results have proved to be very promising, although at the moment there are still concerns about the effects of these fungi on non-target, often beneficial insects, such as pollinators in the environment. Similarly, natural populations of microscopic worm-like 'nematodes', which are able to infect and kill ticks, are being investigated as biological control agents. Such fungal and nematode preparations will eventually add to the array of tools available for tick control, perhaps in an integrated pest management approach, combined with chemical control methods as appropriate.

Novel approaches

Away from the mainstream methods of tick control, there are a number of novel approaches which are met with varying degrees of enthusiasm around the world. The availability of tick repellents to use on livestock is limited, although several studies have indicated the potential benefits of using tick-repellent grasses and plants such as *Melinis minutiflora* (molasses grass or stinkgrass), *Stylosanthes* species (pencil flower) and *Cassia absus* (wild liquorice). A further idea for tick repellents has come out of research in the USA following the observation that a number of mammals and birds appear to 'anoint' themselves with chemicals produced by millipedes as defensive secretions. These chemicals, grouped in a class called benzoquinones, have been shown both to repel ticks and to inhibit their climbing behaviour. Perhaps they provide the animals some protection from questing ticks? Further research will no doubt identify the active chemicals and assess their potential as commercial tick repellents.

Other approaches have included exploiting the tick's own resource-finding behaviour. The two most important activities for a tick are mating and feeding, and both of these are regulated by environmental cues. For blood feeding, ticks latch onto warm, smelly cues which resemble a bloodmeal host, whereas mating tends to be regulated by chemicals, or 'pheromones' produced by the ticks themselves, helping different sexes to recognise each other and to differentiate between species. Over the years, scientists have experimented with both natural and synthetic attractants and pheromones for tick control, often in combination with pesticides. For example, in the Caribbean some control of the cayenne tick is attained by the combination of a natural attractant with a pesticide in an ear tag—attracting the ticks to the tag, from which they pick up a dose of the chemical. In theory at least, this practice was anticipated to save in the order of $1 billion annually on tick control. Unfortunately, widespread success has yet to be recognised through this method, which is most probably linked to the individual behaviour of target species and perhaps highlights how much more we need to improve our understanding of these extremely efficient and successful arthropod pests.

The wider view

Improving vaccines and methods of tick control can only be one part of a control programme. For effective tick and tick-borne disease control, both farmers and advisors need to be educated; for example, to accept the benefits gained from both boosting immunity to tick-borne diseases and from achieving a degree of host resistance through more targeted applications of tick-control measures. This is particularly the case since tick-borne disease-control has mainly become the concern of individual producers in many African countries. For a long time tick-control has been regarded as a national concern, resulting in the provision of communal dips by governments. However, with a change of policy to practice minimal dipping and maintain a level of stability in tick populations, individuals need to know the cost and possible risks of each tick-control initiative, and these need to be weighed against the potential gains from improved milk and meat production. Only then can a comprehensive plan be developed for a sustainable tick and tick-borne disease programme.

Wildlife

Most of this chapter has concentrated on livestock, perhaps understandably, given the significant economic impact that ticks can have on our major food animals. Wildlife, however, act as important reservoir hosts for many tick-borne diseases, and indeed there is a large body of evidence to suggest that tick infestations in a variety of mammals and birds can have significant impacts on both the survival of their populations, as well as their behaviour. Sudden collapses in the populations of animals such as rabbits, hares or colonial nesting seabirds can often be explained by tick epidemics, while ticks can cause certain animals to flee from their nesting or breeding grounds, abandoning their eggs and young.

On British moors and upland farms, not only are sheep susceptible to tick-transmitted louping ill, but red grouse (*Lagopus lagopus scoticus*) are as well, with often serious economic consequences. Research by the Game Conservancy Trust in Scotland has shown that tick-transmitted louping ill can reduce the breeding success of red grouse, and also kill up to 80% of their chicks if they become infected. Of great concern in this case is that, with increases in the number of host animals such as red deer, and warmer winters encouraging increased tick activity, the problem could escalate—in 1985, 4% of grouse chicks surveyed had ticks, but by 2003 this number had risen to 92%! More recently, ornithologists are talking about the louping ill virus infecting a wider range of birds, including important ground-nesting waders that share the grouse's habitat, such as the lapwing, the rare golden plover and the curlew. A radio-tracking programme during autumn 2004 is expected to reveal the possible impact of louping ill on these birds, to allow a plan of action to be devised.

The commonest mammalian wildlife tick hosts in upland Britain are red deer, *Cervus elaphus*, mountain hares, *Lepus timidus*, and rabbits, *Oryctolagus cuniculus*. Although they can be natural reservoirs for louping ill, these groups show no signs of the disease. Roe deer, *Capreolus capreolus*, are also an excellent reservoir of *Ehrlichia phagocytophila*, the cause of tick-borne fever in sheep in upland Britain. Culling programmes of these animals will often have as one of their stated objectives tick control to reduce the threat of tick-transmitted disease to sheep and grouse. These strategies are not always successful, due to a number of misconceptions, such as a failure to take account of alternative hosts (a whole range of small mammals are potential culprits) and a misunderstanding of the extent to which the ranges of species, both those controlled and those protected, might overlap.

Even without the threat of disease transmission, birds in particular can suffer significantly merely from the attachment of ticks. This is particularly the case with seabirds, which nest often in huge colonies and use the same site from year to year, behaviour which presumably helps the tick population to become established. A record of 20,000 ticks per square foot has been recorded for a colony of terns in Florida, and heavy tick infestations have been held responsible for the reduction through nest failure of brown pelicans on the Texas coast to just 100 birds, from a population which once numbered 5000. Desertion of a cliff-side colony of birds is not uncommon when ticks become such a problem, with disastrous consequences for the eggs and young left behind. Even King Penguins don't escape—a recent study of these birds on sub-Antarctic islands revealed a lower incubating success in tick-infested areas and a lower success in rearing their chicks. The loss of blood from young birds (and also from the young of a number of small mammals such as voles and shrews) through heavy tick infestations can have catastrophic effects, and can be fatal. Even large mammals are vulnerable, particularly those that are farmed, since higher stocking-rates often result in a higher rate of parasitism. In New Zealand, a study with farmed deer has demonstrated that blood loss caused by as few as 30 adult ticks can result in anaemia and a reduced weight gain, with deaths being reported with heavier tick infestations. Closer to home, it has been suggested that red deer in Scotland roll on the ground in areas of dry or dusty soil in an attempt to remove attached ticks.

Where there is wildlife there is often the outdoor rambler, the sportsman or the enthusiastic 'watcher', be it as an individual or within a group, possibly as part of the increasingly popular 'wildlife tourism' trend. Ramblers and more serious walkers should always be aware of the possibility of picking up ticks from the undergrowth, particularly in areas where sheep and deer abound. In relation to the increasing concern about Lyme disease in the UK, many walkers' groups and other outdoor organisations have issued warnings to their members about the need to be vigilant. Simple measures have been shown to successfully reduce the likelihood of ticks on clothing becoming attached to the skin. These include wearing long white trousers either tucked into socks or worn over long boots, regular personal inspections and brushing, together with the use of repellents. Reducing exposure to ticks by keeping to clear, wide paths, away from dense vegetation, has also recently been shown to help the casual walker in Ireland.

With deer-stalking there is an increased risk of coming into contact with ticks; deer-stalkers who regularly frequent deer-occupied habitats and handle carcases are a very high-risk group, because their encounters with ticks are common. Very active personal de-ticking and protection is required to reduce this risk. Both workers and recreational visitors in these environments, many of whom may have been unaware of the threat of ticks, should always be informed of the effectiveness of personal de-ticking behaviours. Nymphs and larvae of the sheep tick, *Ixodes ricinus*, also commonly feed on bats, and those workers and volunteers who regularly handle bats should be alert to the possibility of ticks attaching to them. Bird-watchers too are at risk, as they crawl through undergrowth and sit for many hours often in tick-infested hides, waiting patiently for a new sighting.

Wildlife tourism often involves an expert who will guide you through a range of habitats in search of both common and rare wildlife. Alongside planning the tour and dealing with clients, tour leaders are required to provide health and safety information. One site in Scotland suggests that a trip through a Highland bog in the summer involves a very high risk of midge bites; clearly ticks lurking in the undergrowth should also be added to the list of potential hazards.

8
TICKS AND OUR PETS: A GROWING PROBLEM

Threats of ticks to our pets

- Cats, dogs and horses are frequently exposed to ticks, although the majority of ticks are harmless to our pets. 🕷

- When tick-transmitted diseases do occur in our pets, they can be life-threatening if not caught early.

- The most obvious warning signs that our pets may have been bitten by a disease-carrying tick include fever, lameness, loss of appetite, a sudden onset of pain in their legs or body, arthritis or swelling in their joints, lethargy or a cough.

- Most tick-borne diseases do not occur naturally in the UK, although Lyme disease is an exception, caused by the same bacterium as in humans.

- The increase in pets travelling abroad through travel schemes has increased their exposure to foreign tick-borne diseases which, if not picked up quickly, can be lethal.

- A combination of safe insecticides and physical methods can help protect our pets from ticks.

The Background

It is probably true to say that, over the past two decades, we have become increasingly aware of the potential threat of diseases transmitted by insects and related arthropods. A combination of reasons is probably responsible for this, including increased overseas travel and climate change bringing previously 'exotic' species and their associated diseases into closer proximity to Man, together with advances in both biotechnology and medical sciences, allowing the correct identification and diagnosis of previously undiagnosed 'viral-like' illnesses. For biting flies, one of the most publicised recent examples has been mosquito-transmitted West Nile virus, originally found in Africa, the Middle East and West Asia, but now permanently established in the Western hemisphere, including North America. Tick-transmitted Lyme disease has also hit the headlines since its first description in humans in 1975, and is now recognised by the US Center of Disease Control and Prevention as the most common arthropod-borne disease of humans in the United States. Given our often-close relationships with our pets, together with improved veterinary diagnosis, it is no surprise that similar conditions are beginning to be recognised in our closest of friends. Indeed, in some cases a certain amount of paranoia appears to have broken out. For example, amongst cat owners in the United States, increasing concern about Lyme disease is leading to a growing trend of keeping 'house cats'; i.e. confining them indoors rather than letting them roam out-of-doors and possibly coming into contact with ticks.

Which species of tick?

Several types of ticks are commonly found on our pets in the UK, and this section will mainly concentrate on perhaps the favourite pets—dogs and cats. The problem species of tick include the ubiquitous sheep tick, *Ixodes ricinus*, which is also known as the deer tick or castor bean tick—actually, the Romans named the castor bean after the tick, thinking that the seed resembled a blood-filled tick. As already highlighted in previous chapters, this species infests not only our pets but also humans and other animals. Cats and dogs may also pick up 'hedgehog ticks' and the aptly named 'British dog ticks' (also known as fox ticks), and 'brown dog ticks'. Whereas the sheep tick is a free-living tick species which actively searches for its host by climbing up to the top of vegetation, where it 'quests' in search for a passing animal, in contrast, hedgehog ticks live in sheltered places such as kennels or burrows. This species frequently infests pets in large numbers when they are exposed to them—it is often the villain when dogs become repeatedly infested with ticks, particularly around the head area. Cats are also susceptible to this species; during a recent survey carried out by vets across the UK and Northern Ireland, around 40% of the tick samples collected came from cats, with the hedgehog tick being most commonly found.

Where and when?

Pets are not only exposed to ticks in wooded areas and heathland; they can equally pick them up in our own gardens, in parks, from animal burrows and also kennels. Traditionally there are two peaks to the tick season; spring and autumn, although ticks can remain a problem throughout the summer (effectively from April to October) and often beyond, depending on the weather conditions, with optimal conditions for tick reproduction and survival being warm temperatures and high humidity.

Ticks and your pet's health

Remember, each feeding stage of a tick's life (i.e. larva, nymph and adult) requires a blood meal in order to reach the next stage. Estimates of tick densities are difficult to make, but given the high numbers that can be found, particularly in close proximity to their definitive hosts (deer and sheep for the sheep tick) and with estimates of infection rates of between 10 and 30%, it is certainly worth being alert to ticks attaching to your pet. In the UK, although most of the tick-transmitted diseases are rare in dogs and cats, when they do occur they can have very serious consequences—even life threatening. A tick bite can be fatal to your pet. If your dog or cat becomes ill after being in a tick-infested area, remember to tell your vet.

Tick infestation: what problems can you expect?

Ticks can cause problems in your pet both from their physical attachment and also from the diseases that they can potentially transmit. In particular, tick-transmitted infections are an emerging problem in dogs. As well as causing serious illness in tropical and semi-tropical regions, they are becoming increasingly recognised as the cause of disease in dogs in temperate and urban regions. What are the factors responsible for this? Most probably a combination of a number of developments, including the movement of infected dogs into previously disease-free areas, the expansion of the tick's range into urban and semi-urban areas across the world and improvements in disease diagnosis.

The majority of animals will never show any signs of distress as a result of tick attachment, but in a few, effects can include irritation, local infection, inflammation and even hypersensitive (allergic) reactions to tick bites.

The majority of tick-borne diseases are thought to be exotic to the UK (that is, they are foreign diseases not normally present in the UK but which, if introduced, have the potential to have serious health implications). However, Lyme disease and a form of ehrlichiosis are already endemic in the UK, both being transmitted by the commonest tick in the UK, the sheep tick *Ixodes ricinus*.

Lyme disease in pets

Although Lyme disease is relatively uncommon in the UK, the general view is that hotter summers are seeing an increase in the disease. However, it is still frequently overlooked by vets (as well as doctors) who are unfamiliar with its symptoms. Following the naming of the disease in the United States in 1975 after an outbreak of human Lyme disease in Old Lyme, Connecticut, the reported incidences in both pets and humans increased during the 1980s. Although Lyme disease is less well known in British veterinary circles, it is well documented in American pet magazines and journals, and there are literally hundreds of websites detailing the symptoms, how to protect your pet and, if necessary, how the disease can be treated.

As in humans, Lyme disease in cats and dogs is caused by the spiral-shaped bacterium, *Borrelia burgdorferi* (or other closely related species). Bacterial transmission to the host starts approximately 36 to 48 hours after tick attachment—and so it is important to remove ticks as soon as you see them on your animal. From the site of tick attachment, the bacteria multiply and migrate through tissues, invading the joints nearest to the bite site first. In contrast to the infection in humans, where three different stages are well known (including the characteristic skin rash), the disease in dogs is primarily an acute or sub-acute arthritis, with approximately 5% of all infected dogs becoming ill. The most obvious and common symptom of Lyme disease in dogs is a recurring lameness—it is usually a front leg that is affected, and this lameness is often associated with an enlarged lymph node on the same shoulder. Together with hot, painful joints, walking, playing or even being touched can be very uncomfortable for the dog (or cat). This lameness and associated muscle and joint pain may be intermittent (perhaps associated with the migration of the Lyme bacteria around the body), often with several episodes that shift between different limbs and persist for days or even weeks. Other clinical signs are appetite loss and general depression. Fortunately, antibiotic treatment is very effective during this stage of illness.

If Lyme disease is untreated during the first acute stage, it may move into the sub-clinical phase, with the animal not showing any apparent symptoms. As long as the animal is not subjected to something that causes undue stress (e.g. other infections, immuno-deficiency, surgery, excessive work or pregnancy), this phase can last for months or even years, with the parasite effectively living with the host in a state of equilibrium. However, if this balance is disturbed, the disease organism can quickly gain the upper hand, pushing the animal into the chronic stage of illness. By this stage, the disease may have entered one or a number of organs (such as the bone-marrow, spleen, heart, kidney or liver), making it much harder to treat successfully. In particular, the animal's immune capabilities are likely to be impaired (including its ability to make antibodies to combat the disease) and neurological symptoms such as fits, aggression and other behavioural changes have been reported. Sometimes, when a cat or dog has entered the chronic stage of Lyme disease, there is no form of effective treatment and death can occur. It must be stressed, however, that very few tick bites lead to such serious complications and, in fact, the majority of cases of Lyme disease are asymptomatic or sub-clinical—that is, the animal appears healthy.

Horses can also become infected with the bacteria causing Lyme disease, with infection rates in horses being as high as 50% across Europe. However, the vast majority of infections are asymptomatic, and clinical cases are rare, even if some may be missed because of the non-specific nature of the symptoms. Where clinical symptoms do occur, these consist mainly of fatigue, fever, stiffness, swollen joints and eye infections. However, unequivocal diagnosis of equine Lyme disease is very difficult.

Ehrlichiosis in pets

Ehrlichiosis is an infectious disease caused by the group of bacteria *Ehrlichia*, named after the German microbiologist Paul Ehrlich in 1945. It affects dogs, sheep, horses and cattle and is also being increasingly recognised in humans, as outlined in Chapter 4. In the UK it is primarily transmitted by *Ixodes ricinus* (the sheep tick). In humans, ehrlichiosis exists as two clinically similar illnesses: human monocytic ehrlichiosis (HME), caused by *Ehrlichia chaffeensis*, and human granulocytic ehrlichiosis (HGE), caused by *Ehrlichia equi* and *Ehrlichia phagocytophila*. Both are typically characterised by fever, headache, pains in the muscles and chills.

Many species of the genus *Ehrlichia* will infect dogs, with the added complication that the bone marrow is often infected —i.e. the animal's white blood cells—which greatly reduces the performance of the immune system. Symptoms include fever, depression, seizures, meningitis, lameness and joint swelling, weight-loss, and loss of appetite. Death is not uncommon. It is a difficult disease to diagnose, with dogs steadily becoming more and more lethargic and losing increasing amounts of weight until the more serious conditions associated with immune deficiency kick in. One American vet estimates that canine ehrlichiosis accounts for 10-20% of all 'ADR' cases he sees—dogs that 'Ain't Doing Right'!

The first recognition of ehrlichiosis in dogs was associated with *Ehrlichia canis* infection in Algeria in 1935, and historically, the disease was of great significance during the Vietnam War, when it was thought to be responsible for the death of hundreds of military dogs. Associated with this, some scientists believe that the disease made its way into the United States when the primary carrier of the disease in this area, the brown dog tick, hitched a ride from Vietnam back to the mainland on American soldiers.

One reason for military dogs being singled out is that German shepherds appear to be particularly susceptible to the disease, often developing fatal haemorrhage in the late chronic phase of the illness, whereas mixed breeds and, for some reason, beagles generally appear not to be. One recent American study found detectable antibodies to *E. canis* in 11% of military working dogs internationally and 57% of civilian dogs in the United States.

E. canis is not an endemic species in the UK, where most cases of canine ehrlichiosis are caused by *Ehrlichia phagocytophlia* (as in humans), which is also responsible for the condition known as tick-borne fever (TBF), which is an enzootic condition (i.e. it is constantly present at a low level) among sheep in upland areas of the UK, and is transmitted by *Ixodes* ticks. Domestic sheep are thought to act as the main reservoir host for the disease organism, with cattle, rodents and deer also being competent reservoir hosts.

Although reports of ehrlichiosis in dogs are not common, this is most probably due to a failure to diagnose. In a recent letter to the *Veterinary Record*, veterinary surgeons from the Universities of Bristol and Edinburgh reported six cases of *Ehrlichia phagocytophlia* in dogs, all of which were resident in the UK and had not travelled abroad—two from Suffolk and one each from Gloucester, Bristol, Glamorgan and Fife. The clinical findings apparently were consistent with meningitis and/or polyarthritis, with fever, lethargy, muscle stiffness, spinal and/or joint pain. It was suggested that this may have been analogous to a 'tick-borne fever' syndrome reported in working dogs in northern Scotland in 1996—apparently such cases continue to occur in Scotland, even though they remain unpublished. The condition is treatable with antibiotics; in the acute stage of the disease most dogs will respond to treatment within 24 to 48 hours and have a favourable prognosis. Chronic infections are harder to treat.

Horses can also become infected with ehrlichiosis, with the agent responsible being *Ehrlichia risticii*. This is a recently defined disease of horses (which is also called Potomac horse fever). It is an infectious, non-contagious, seasonal disease, seen chiefly in northern California but also recorded in several other North American States, as well as in parts of Europe and South America. The incidence peaks in the summer months, with approximately 30% of cases proving to be fatal. Clinical signs include lethargy, appetite loss, fever, colic, diarrhoea, and laminitis (a painful condition of the feet). Usually a horse will show one or a combination of symptoms but rarely all of them. Although ticks have been suspected as the vectors of this disease, it now seems more likely that it is carried by freshwater snails, and that infective parasites are picked up by horses whilst drinking from streams and ponds.

Jet-setting pets: avoiding the travel bug

Since February 2000, our pets (dogs, cats and ferrets!) have been able to accompany us on holiday to certain destinations through the 'Pet Travel Scheme' (PETS), which also allows pet animals from certain countries to enter the UK without quarantine as long as they meet the rules. The scheme, originally covering a number of European countries, has now been extended to cover North America and other long-haul destinations, such as Japan, New Zealand and Fiji. With new EU regulations coming into force from the beginning of July 2004, not only have the numbers of countries which qualify for the scheme been increased but also the types of animal which qualify—including rodents, domestic rabbits, birds (except certain poultry), ornamental tropical fish, invertebrates (except bees and crustaceans), amphibians and reptiles, although the exact requirements relating to these within the scheme have yet to be released by Brussels.

Despite the regulations relating to the Pet Travel Scheme (including vaccination against rabies and treatment for ticks and tapeworms), increasing numbers of British pets are catching potentially lethal diseases on foreign holidays, as travelling with our pets becomes more and more popular. In 2000, 14,549 pet cats and dogs entered England under PETS. This figure rose to 136,934 in 2003. Concurrently, exotic tick-borne diseases have shown increases of about 100 per cent according to UK veterinary schools. The tick-transmitted diseases that produce greatest concern are babesiosis and ehrlichiosis. Babesiosis can cause a pet's death within days, whereas some of the other diseases have much longer incubation periods—sometimes years. Visiting British pets are particularly vulnerable compared with foreign pets, since they have no immunity to the infections and there are no vaccinations available.

Victims include Hamie, the 16-month-old West Highland terrier from Tyneside, who died after contracting tick-borne babesiosis on holiday in the Dordogne, leaving behind a shattered family. A number of other canine visitors to France have returned with babesiosis, in addition to dogs that have entered the UK under PETS from Thailand (*via* Germany) and Japan, whilst dogs entering through the scheme from Greece have been diagnosed with ehrlichiosis.

Increased awareness

Most of these exotic diseases are picked up on beaches and in woods and gardens in Mediterranean countries, including France, Spain, Italy and Greece. A visit to these areas can be as dangerous to animals as a trip to the tropics can be for humans—perhaps more so, since human diseases such as malaria are extremely high profile and there are a number of precautionary measures available. A huge problem still exists for vets in detecting these diseases, but this is beginning to be tackled by experts in the field—for example, the Liverpool University Veterinary Department has established a diagnostic service called 'Testapet' to assist UK vets. In addition, in March 2003 the Department for Environment, Food & Rural Affairs (Defra) launched DACTARI (Dog and Cat Travel and Risk Information), which is a national voluntary reporting scheme established to find out about the occurrence of exotic diseases in dogs and cats in Great Britain. It involves both the British Veterinary Association (BVA) and the British Small Animal Veterinary Association (BSAVA) and provides guidance for both vets and pet owners. An annual report is produced and the findings are also published regularly in the veterinary press.

What can we expect?

Babesiosis in dogs is caused by the same protozoan parasites of the genus *Babesia* responsible for the disease in wildlife, as described previously. The principal agent in dogs is *Babesia canis*. It is effectively a disease of the red blood cells and results in acute symptoms such as fever, loss of appetite and general deterioration. Shock, coma or death after less than a day of lethargy and loss of appetite can occur. It occurs in most southern European countries but is particularly widespread in most regions of France and has been seen as far north as Paris and parts of Belgium, Germany and the Netherlands. There is no vaccine available in the UK and complete cures are rare unless the disease is caught in the very early stages, although this is difficult, since in many cases the onset and death are so rapid.

Ehrlichiosis has been described above. Outside of the UK, *Ehrlichia canis* is the commonest cause of the disease, with a worldwide distribution in many tropical and sub-tropical areas including southern Europe and the Mediterranean. It is particularly widespread in Mediterranean countries, with 'hotspots' including Portugal, Italy and Spain—in addition to areas of Holland, Germany and Belgium. Transmission of the infective bacteria to the animal occurs within one or two days of tick attachment, resulting in fever and potentially problems with their immune system and bleeding disorders.

Bacterial organisms in the genus *Rickettsia* also exist worldwide and are responsible for human diseases such as Q fever and Rocky Mountain spotted fever (RMSF). The primary species that causes disease in dogs is also infectious to humans, *Rickettsia rickettsii*, the agent of Rocky Mountain spotted fever in North and South America—its name relating to the fact that it was first described in humans from Montana and Idaho in the late nineteenth century. Symptoms in dogs infected with *R. rickettsii* are similar to those suffering from ehrlichiosis, with a rapid and severe disease course. Fever occurs 4–5 days after the tick bite, with the clinical symptoms progressing towards a range of organ malfunctions. Although very similar to the canine ehrlichiae, RMSF differs in that the duration of the illness with *R. rickettsia* is much shorter (usually lasting for about 2 weeks), it has a more rapid onset and, also, lacks a chronic phase. This is due to the animal developing protective immunity, which explains why RMSF most often affects younger (less than 3-years-old) dogs, which have not yet had a chance to do this. Other tick-transmitted *Rickettsia* spp. that infect dogs are generally non-pathogenic (i.e. do not cause disease), but dogs are considered reservoir hosts, for example for the rickettsial organism causing Q fever, which is a significant public health threat in five continents and of veterinary importance to livestock.

A growing problem?

It is estimated that about 300 dogs from the UK catch diseases abroad each year. Although this number seems relatively small compared to the numbers of animals actually travelling under the PETS scheme, it is likely that these figures represent only the tip of the iceberg; many more cases may be undiagnosed or unreported, with diseases like babesiosis often killing before an accurate diagnosis can be made.

While opening up all kinds of new opportunities for us and our pets, it is perhaps still worthwhile asking whether or not the family cat or dog really needs to go with us on holiday, and if they do, they should be checked on return if they show any sign of illness. Furthermore, with an ever-increasing list of animals that will be able to cross European borders and those further afield, there will be no limit to the list of arthropod-transmitted diseases our pets could become exposed to.

Can I catch tick-transmitted diseases from my pet?

It is bad enough for your dog to catch an exotic (or home-grown) disease from a tick feeding upon it, but would it be possible for the disease to be passed on to other animals back in Britain—or possibly to humans? To date, there is no evidence that this has happened. It had been speculated that *B. burgdorferi* (the agent causing Lyme disease) in the saliva or urine of infected dogs might be transmissible to humans. However, experiments to test this hypothesis, in which infected and uninfected dogs have been kept in close contact for extended periods, have failed to provide any evidence of urine or saliva transmission and infection. In addition, so far, there has been no evidence produced of human infection resulting from contact with infected dogs. The only exception might be if dogs brought only loosely attached ticks into the home, which subsequently dropped off and transferred to humans.

How to protect your pet

Insecticides and repellents

Protection of our pets against ticks is much the same as protecting ourselves. There are numerous websites and fact sheets which recommend that you should keep your pet animal away from long grass and areas where ticks are likely to lie in wait for unsuspecting animals, but in practical terms, this is virtually impossible. You can provide them with some protection, however, through the use of a number of safe insecticidal preparations that may be obtained from a vet. These are usually liquid and applied once a month to a small area of the cat or dog's skin, after which they spread over the animal's body *via* the oil on its skin and kill ticks before they get a chance to cause any harm. Such 'spot-on' or 'pour-on' preparations are beginning to replace repellent and insecticidal sprays, collars, powders and dips, which contain a variety of synthetic chemicals. Although these repel ticks to some degree, there is also debate about the effectiveness and safety of the collars, to both your pet and yourself.

Pet collars for protecting against fleas and ticks have long been impregnated with a group of insecticides called 'organophosphates' (or 'OPs'), which have been sold widely;

more than a billion dollars a year are spent on flea and tick products, the majority of these containing insecticides. OPs interfere with nerve transmission to such an extent that they actually kill insects. However, continual exposure can also be harmful both to people (particularly children) and pets, and there is a steady move towards the use of safer products, together with easy physical measures, such as frequent washing and combing of your pet. Alternatives to OPs which are incorporated into products sold by our vets include fipronil and imidacloprid. Both of these products are applied topically to the skin and within 24 hours the products spread *via* natural oils to all areas of the body, remaining in the oil (sebaceous) glands and hair follicles for up to three months. They are not absorbed into the blood. Just like OPs, they result in tick death through interference with the nervous system, but unlike OPs, both compounds appear to be safe in their mechanism of action and in short-term toxicity studies. These two products really revolutionised external parasite control on pets, particularly of fleas, due to their quick action, but with the added benefit of being effective against ticks as well. Now, however, there is a further group of new products, which are highly effective, non-toxic and applied as a single spot-on. These are based on a class of insecticides called avermectins (primarily 'selemectin', marketed under a variety of names), which act by targeting a range of biochemical sites in the parasite to cause their death. These are heralded as being as close to a one-stop-shop total parasite control product as you can get, since they are absorbed into your pet's system and effectively protect against internal and external parasites, including intestinal roundworms, fleas, ticks and mites. Also, unlike the previous two products, they don't leave a greasy spot on your pet's back, which so often is forgotten when you handle your animal! The only apparent disadvantages of the avermectins are that firstly, they are not quite as instantaneous in killing as other treatments, and secondly, because they are absorbed into the pet's system, some people will be worried about potential toxicity, although more than ten years of testing have shown no grounds for concern. They have a wide margin of safety in mammals and are considered safe in breeding male and female dogs and cats, together with pregnant and lactating dogs and cats. When used in combination with physical measures, the safety and effectiveness of these newer chemical products makes the continued use of pet products containing OPs and their associated risks for humans and pets alike, unnecessary.

You may still prefer the natural approach to tick control on your pets and a whole range of herbal collars is available, containing essential oils such as citronella, rosemary and rose geranium. There are also an equal number of home-grown tick remedies. These including adding a tablespoon of organic apple cider vinegar to the pet's water bowl, putting a drop of lemon oil or rosemary oil on their collar, dabbing lavender oil between the pet's shoulder blades and even grating fresh garlic into their food—apparently it makes the animal taste unpleasant to ticks!

Once you have decided upon a tick-treatment, care should always be taken when using it, depending on whether it is a dog or cat you are trying to protect and the age of the animal, and you should always check with your vet. Also, it is not advised to 'double up' on insecticides or repellents, and if a vet has prescribed a topical once-a-month treatment, it is probably best to consult them first before using additional products.

Vaccines

There is a vaccine approved for use in dogs for Lyme disease prevention, but it is not licensed in the UK and there is considerable debate regarding its effectiveness. The vaccine will only prevent infection in dogs vaccinated before any exposure to the Lyme bacteria, making it only helpful for dogs such as puppies and dogs from non-endemic areas travelling to endemic areas. Vaccination against the disease is highly controversial. Most experts appear to come down against vaccinating, suggesting that since Lyme disease in the dog is an infection from which over 90% of infected dogs will never get ill, and that the 5% to 10% that do get sick can be easily treated with a safe inexpensive course of antibiotics, vaccination is of questionable value.

Whichever route is chosen, as for our own protection, vigilance is of most importance. Keep a look out for ticks on your cat or dog and carefully pick off those you find—remembering how small the larvae and nymphs can be—and take care not to crush them, potentially releasing infective particles. To remove, use tweezers gently to grasp the tick as close to the cat or dog's skin as possible and gently pull away from the skin, cleaning the area afterwards with antiseptic if your pet will allow! Of greatest importance, if your pet becomes ill after travelling outside the UK and you think that it may have come into contact with ticks, you should tell your vet immediately.

Climate change: what does the future hold for tick-transmitted diseases?

There are numerous reports that ticks and their associated diseases are on the increase in the USA, UK and Western Europe, with the national press in particular picking up on the potential horrors of increases in Lyme disease. A complex set of factors influences how tick populations fluctuate, and subsequently, how patterns of disease infection change. One of these factors is, undoubtedly, climate, with recent and predicted changes very likely to remould the ecology of tick populations. Warmer temperatures increase their reproductive and feeding rates, together with the efficiency of disease transmission. In addition, related changes in rainfall and humidity may alter the suitability of local habitats for resting ticks. Improved tick survival has already been recorded, with warmer, wetter weather no doubt contributing. This can only help to underline the importance of vigilance in relation to ticks and tick-transmitted diseases, and the threats to ourselves, our livestock and our pets.

9
FUTURE PROSPECTS

Ticks—and how little we know

- The relationship between ticks, as parasites, and their hosts, as a source of blood-meals, is an ancient one. No mammal or bird has evolved complete protection against ticks or tick-borne disease.

- We are not able to predict, with reliability, the spread of tick-borne disease, particularly under changing climates.

- We understand little of how ticks survive in the environment when not feeding. Could this be the key to controlling tick numbers?

- We know little of how ticks interact with small wild mammals. Is this the key to tick success?

- Tick control, in human health, will depend greatly on increasing public awareness of ticks and their diseases.

- One aspect has general agreement in Europe—ticks thrive in warm, wet climates.

Most parasites and their hosts have a long and close relationship. They have evolved together. One of the theories underlying our understanding of evolution is that parasites and their hosts are locked into a perpetual arms race. Parasites continuously seek new ways to breach the host's ever-evolving resistance. Simultaneously, for the host there is a never-ending search for new defences against parasites. At any one time, some hosts will have genes which make them better able to resist parasites and they will breed to produce resistant offspring. Other individuals without this advantage will more readily succumb to being parasitized. The theory runs to the core of biological evolution and holds that parasites, indeed, drive sexual reproduction (involving the acquisition of new genes for one's offspring) and, in time, over many generations, will result in the evolution of new species (an individual with sufficiently different genes to vary significantly from its ancestors). Ticks fit the theories of evolution well.

Ticks have been actively challenging mammals, reptiles and birds for many tens of millions of years. We can also say, with some confidence, that no mammal or bird has yet evolved which is wholly resistant to ticks or to tick-borne diseases. Seen against that background, we have to face up to the fact that our 21st century attempts to control ticks by pesticides, pheromones, manipulation of host or habitat are not likely to seriously disturb the age-old evolutionary relationship between ticks and their hosts. At very best we may succeed in tilting the tick-host relationship to favour the health of our livestock. We can provide some answers to the ravages of tick-borne diseases of humans. But it is arrogance to think that we can make any lasting impact on the close relationship that has long existed between ticks, their hosts and tick-borne micro-organisms.

The way forward

Today we recognize that tick control through pesticide application, through host eradication campaigns or through methods of biological control have their limitations, avermectins included. Tick control using pheromones, while showing promise in small scale short-term experiments, has yet to be proven in wider trials.

Vaccination programmes have worked well to control many animal diseases, but may be expensive and some require repeated administration. However, advances in molecular biology make it likely that more effective and cheaper vaccines will be developed, at least against the most economically important diseases. Already molecular vaccines have been developed to control bovine and ovine tick-borne fevers in heartwater and redwater of cattle.

While we wait for new technological advances, an important development in the war against ticks in recent years has been what is called integrated pest control. This means tackling a population of ticks at several different levels. The control of Texas cattle fever in the USA and east coast fever in southern Africa, for example, is largely due to the combined effects of the use of pesticides, the import and breeding of tick-resistant breeds of cattle and strict control over livestock movement. Reliance on just one main method of control has proved, time after time, to be short-sighted, and it is likely that integrated pest management will become the standard, particularly in large-scale farming.

The major contribution to tick control throughout the last hundred years, however, has come from a greater awareness of ticks among farmers and the public, as well as our improved understanding of tick biology, of tick and host ecology and disease transmission. This alone has done much to improve animal welfare. There are, however, many outstanding questions to be answered affecting not just the welfare of our livestock but also human health.

Paramount is our inability to predict, with any great accuracy, the spread of tick-borne disease and to forecast new epidemics. This is not just a problem of range or ranch farming in the tropics, it could become a significant problem in western Europe if recent patterns of climate change continue. Underlying our inability to predict changes in tick-borne disease and tick behaviour, is our woefully sketchy idea of how ticks interact with wildlife. This is particularly true of the European sheep tick, which relies on a variety of small wild mammals to sustain its early development, a reliance which ultimately determines the size of the tick population. Effective integration of pest control methods may well depend on understanding how ticks behave when not on the backs of sheep or cattle or the legs of walkers. In addition, despite a hundred years of experience with outbreaks of tick-borne diseases in places as dissimilar as Montana and Harare, Adelaide or Galloway, we still fail to predict epidemics. In part this is because we lack a full picture of the distribution of many tick-borne diseases, veterinary and medical. This information is, perhaps, the key to disease forecasting.

Although ticks, in terms of economics, are primarily a problem for livestock, it may be that the approach—and the research funding—to answering these outstanding questions will yet come through our concerns over ticks in relation to human health. Animal health is not generally an issue which concerns the public at large, but when there is a link between animal and human health, attitudes do change. It may well be that recent concerns over Lyme disease, not itself a significant scourge of livestock, will do much to generate the search for new solutions to the problem of living with ticks.

Ultimately, however, as far as human health is concerned there can be no substitute for public health education—for the individual to be aware of the potential dangers of tick bites—and for the individual to balance worries over tick-borne disease with a commonsense approach to health during work and recreation in rural areas.

Finally, almost anything that can be written about ticks and tick-borne diseases today will need to be revised in the years to come, if and when climate change becomes a significant factor. We already know from detailed records that tick numbers have increased in several study areas over several years. One such study by the Game Conservancy Trust in Britain has shown a five-fold increase in tick numbers on chicks of red grouse over a 19-year period. One explanation for this is the pattern of wetter and milder winters and wetter springs over the past two decades. Several reports have emerged in recent years implicating changes in weather patterns with the incidence of several tick-borne diseases in continental Europe. While it would be wrong to over-emphasise the findings of any one report, the pattern within the literature that seems to be arising, in the last three or four years, is of increased impact of ticks, expansion of tick populations in size and area, and heightened incidence of tick-borne diseases in western Europe. The indicators for some of these changes point towards alterations in weather patterns that appear to be becoming a feature of the climate over the past decade or more. Warm wet climates favour ticks!

APPENDIX
Ticks of Mainland Britain and its Islands

Note: The list of diseases carried by most ticks described in the table on the following pages may understate the true picture, particularly the long list of diseases transmitted by the sheep tick. In addition, several species of tick are known to carry diseases in continental Europe which have not yet been recorded in Britain. On human biting, the symbol - means that either biting of humans has not been recorded or is uncommon. Finally, there are two or three species which have not yet been recorded in Britain but are present in compatible habitats in France and Germany and which feed on livestock. These ticks could well enter the British list. The common names given here are those used by Hillyard (1996).

APPENDIX
Ticks of Mainland Britain and its Islands

Common name	Zoological name	Main UK habitat	Principal host	Diseases carried	Bites humans
Hard ticks					
Long-legged bat tick	*Ixodes vespertilionis*	Bat caves Wales & SW	Bats	TBE virus	–
Brown dog tick	*Rhipicephalus sanguineus*	Kennels S England	Dogs	Dog babesiosis & rickettsiosis	yes
Ornate cow tick	*Dermacentor reticulatus*	Pastures Wales & SW	Cattle, dog, sheep, horse	Redwater fever, canine babesiosis	yes
Cormorant tick	*Ixodes unicavatus*	Rocky coastal nesting sites	Sea birds	Little known	–
Fox tick	*Ixodes canisuga*	Kennels, lairs UK-wide	Dogs, foxes, badgers, cats	Badger babesiosis	–
Hedgehog tick	*Ixodes hexagonus*	Suburbs to forests	Dogs, cats, small mammals	Lyme disease and others	yes
Marsh tick	*Ixodes apronophorus*	East Anglian marshes	Waterside mammals	Water vole tularemia	–
Northern bird tick	*Ixodes caledonicus*	Nests & roosts in north	Pigeons, seabirds	Little known	–
Passerine tick	*Ixodes frontalis*	Parks, gardens, woods	Migrant & resident birds	Q-fever	–
Puffin tick	*Ixodes rothschildi*	Puffin burrows Wales & SW	Puffins, shearwaters	Several viruses	–

Rabbit tick	*Ixodes ventalloi*	Rabbit burrows SW England	Rabbits, cats, lizards	*Exact virus*	yes
Red sheep tick	*Haemaphysalis punctata*	Pastures Wales & SE	Sheep, cattle, birds	Louping ill Lyme disease	yes
Rodent tick	*Ixodes acuminatus*	Burrows, nests SW England	Small rodents	Lyme disease	yes
Sand martin tick	*Ixodes lividus*	Sand martin burrows	Sand martins, Great tits	RSSE virus	–
Seabird tick	*Ixodes uriae*	Coastal nesting sites	Cliff-nesting sea birds	Lyme disease & many viruses	yes, and painful
Sheep tick	*Ixodes ricinus*	Moist grass & moorland	Many mammals, birds, reptiles	Lyme disease Louping ill	yes
Two-host tick	*Hyalomma marginatum*	Migrant birds from the south	Birds	Haemorrhagic fevers	yes
Tree-hole tick	*Ixodes arboricola*	Nests, roosts S England	Hole-nesting birds	TBE virus	–
Vole tick	*Ixodes trianguliceps*	Forests, rodent nests	Small mammals	Louping ill Lyme disease	yes
Soft ticks					
Marine argasid	*Ornithodoros maritimus*	Coasts	Seabirds esp. gulls	Several viruses	yes
Pigeon tick	*Argas reflexus*	Pigeon roosts SE England	Pigeons, doves, hens	Fowl diseases Lyme disease	yes, and painful
Short-legged bat tick	*Argas vespertilionis*	Caves, house & church roofs	Bats	Bat diseases rabies (?)	yes, and painful

FURTHER READING

Scientific research, medical, veterinary and biological, has generated a large literature on ticks and their associated diseases. Some of this is available on the Internet along with a large number of web sites recording everything from blow-by-blow personal experiences, down-right scare-mongering, through to some well-written, sensible advice from medical and veterinary practitioners. Unfortunately, much the greater majority is written from a north American perspective and may have limited validity in Europe. European ticks, European forms of Lyme disease and the microbial agents causing tick-borne diseases *differ significantly* from those present in the North-East United States. There are principles, practices and advice which are, of course, valid world-wide, but care should be taken when reading the literature, particularly the tick and Lyme disease web sites, which is intended to be read by north American readers.

And for rather more detailed or specialist information:

Axelford JS and Rees DHE (eds) (1993). *Lyme Borreliosis*. Nato Advanced Workshop, Series A Life Sciences, vol 260. Plenum Press, New York.

Benenson AS (1995). *Control of Communicable Diseases Manual*, American Public Health Association, Washington.

Hillyard PD (1996). *Ticks of North-west Europe*, Field Studies Council, Shrewsbury.

Kettle DS (1995). *Medical and Veterinary Entomology*. 2nd edn. CAB International, Wallingford.

Further Reading

Kurtenbach K, de Michelis S, Etti S, Schafer SM, Sewell H-S, Brade V & Kraiczy P (2002) Host Association of Borrelai burgdorferi sensu lato—the key role of host complement. *Trends in Microbiology*, **10**, 74-79.

Lane RS, Piesman J & Burgdorfer W (1991). Lyme borreliosis: relation of its causitive agent to its vector and hosts in North America and Europe. *Annual Reviews of Entomology*, **36**, 587-609.

Nutall, PA *et al* (1994). Adaptations of arboviruses to ticks. *Journal of Medical Entomology*, **31**, 1-9.

Ostfeld, RS (1997) Ecology of Lyme disease risk. *American Scientist*, **85**, 338-341.

Schmidt, K (1997). If you go down to the woods today. *New Scientist*. 15 November 44-48.

Sonenshine DE (1991) *Biology of Ticks*. Vol 1 & 2. Oxford University Press, Oxford.

Steere AC (1989) Lyme disease. *New England Journal of Medicine*, **321**, 586-596.